Vintage Treasures

LITTLE QUILTS FOR REPRODUCTION FABRICS

Pam Buda

Martingale®
Create with Confidence

Vintage Treasures: Little Quilts for Reproduction Fabrics
© 2020 by Pam Buda

Martingale®
19021 120th Ave. NE, Ste. 102
Bothell, WA 98011-9511 USA
ShopMartingale.com

Printed in Hong Kong
25 24 23 22 21 20   8 7 6 5 4 3 2 1

Library of Congress Cataloging-in-Publication Data is available upon request.

ISBN: 978-1-60468-797-2

MISSION STATEMENT

We empower makers who use fabric and yarn to make life more enjoyable.

CREDITS

**PUBLISHER AND
CHIEF VISIONARY OFFICER**
Jennifer Erbe Keltner

CONTENT DIRECTOR
Karen Costello Soltys

DESIGN MANAGER
Adrienne Smitke

MANAGING EDITOR
Tina Cook

PRODUCTION MANAGER
Regina Girard

**ACQUISITIONS AND
DEVELOPMENT EDITOR**
Laurie Baker

**COVER AND
BOOK DESIGNER**
Sara Suttle

TECHNICAL EDITOR
Ellen Pahl

PHOTOGRAPHER
Brent Kane

COPY EDITOR
Sheila Chapman Ryan

ILLUSTRATOR
Sandy Loi

SPECIAL THANKS
*Photography for this book was taken at
Minglewood Lodge in Gretna, Nebraska.*

Contents

Introduction

I'm smitten with small quilts! When I first started quilting, I only made large quilts, but about eight years ago, small quilts grabbed my heart and have never let go. There are so many ways to decorate with small quilts, which is one of the things I enjoy most about making them. Adding a small quilt (or two—or ten!) to a room adds fabric, texture, color, and warmth in a way that only a quilt can. It's fun to look at everyday objects to find new ways for displaying your quilts. Arrange quilts in a wire basket, tack a quilt to a cutting board that leans against the wall, or roll quilts and tuck them into open drawers of a small cabinet.

Small quilts are nothing new, of course. Nineteenth-century quiltmakers made a whole lot of quilts for their children's dolls. Often, a little girl's first attempt at learning to hold a needle and make stitches was to make a quilt for her doll. While most young girls no longer piece tiny quilts, quilters today cherish antique doll quilts. These treasures can be hard to find because they were well used and loved, but we can make our own beloved small quilts.

The 12 little quilts in this book feature a wide array of blocks, sizes, colors, and skill levels for your piecing enjoyment. Would you like to make them all? Why not? You can't have too many small quilts! I regularly rotate my small quilt collection, not only to enjoy them all, but to unfold and refold them so they don't develop permanent creases. I think the definition of decadence for me is not a luscious fudge-filled chocolate cake (well, maybe that too!), but rather a stack of beautiful quilts. Large or small, a pile of quilts displayed on a bench or a chair is something to behold. Think about the time it took to choose the fabric, cut and piece the quilt, then quilt and bind it. Handmade quilts take practice, skill, and education combined with the love you put into every stitch. Those quilts, large or small, are valuable beyond any monetary consideration. A stack of them is guilt-free fabric decadence!

~ *Pam*

Scraps from Home

In a sweet twist on an old-fashioned yo-yo quilt, I stitched yo-yos to a quilted top rather than simply to each other. Both the yo-yos and the flying-geese units make good use of scrap fabrics—our quilting ancestors would approve! The flying-geese border provides a pleasing contrast with the circular yo-yos.

QUILT SIZE: 20" × 20"

FLYING-GEESE SIZE: 1" × 2" | **YO-YO SIZE: 1¼" diameter**

MATERIALS

Yardage is based on 42"-wide fabric.

½ yard of light print for background and flying geese

⅝ yard *total* of assorted medium and dark prints for flying geese and yo-yos (referred to collectively as "dark")

¾ yard of black print for outer border and bias binding

¾ yard of fabric for backing

24" × 24" piece of batting

Template plastic

Hand-quilting thread for yo-yos (optional)

Freezer paper

Fabric glue such as Roxanne's Glue-Baste-It

Chalk pencil

CUTTING

From the light print, cut:

1 square, 12½" × 12½"

2 strips, 1½" × 42"; crosscut into 52 squares, 1½" × 1½"

From the assorted dark prints, cut:

24 rectangles, 1½" × 2½"

From the black print, cut:

2 strips, 4" × 42"; crosscut into:

  2 strips, 4" × 21½"

  2 strips, 4" × 14½"

2¼"-wide bias strips to yield 100"

4 squares, 1" × 1"

OPPOSITE: Designed and pieced by Pam Buda
Quilted by Ronda Dranter

FLYING-GEESE BORDERS

Press all seam allowances as indicated by the arrows.

1. Referring to "Connector Corners" on page 74, draw a diagonal line on the wrong side of two light 1½" squares. Place a marked square on one end of a dark 1½" × 2½" rectangle. Stitch on the marked line. Press, making sure the raw edges of the triangle are aligned with the edges of the rectangle. Trim away the excess corner fabric, leaving a ¼" seam allowance. Press the triangle back in place. Place a marked square on the opposite end of the rectangle and repeat to make a flying-geese unit measuring 1½" × 2½", including seam allowances. Make a total of 24 units.

Make 24 units, 1½" × 2½".

2. Draw a diagonal line from corner to corner on the wrong side of a black 1" square. Place the marked square on the upper-left corner of a light 1½" square. Sew on the marked line. Press, making sure the raw edges of the triangle are aligned with the edges of the square. Trim away the excess corner fabric, leaving a ¼" seam allowance. Press the triangle back in place to make a corner unit measuring 1½" square, including seam allowances. Make four corner units.

Make 4 units, 1½" × 1½".

3. Join six assorted flying-geese units as shown to make a border measuring 1½" × 12½", including seam allowances. Make a total of four borders. Sew a corner unit to each end of two of the borders to make top and bottom borders that measure 1½" × 14½", including seam allowances.

Make 2 borders, 1½" × 12½".

Make 2 borders, 1½" × 14½".

ASSEMBLING THE QUILT

1. Sew the 1½" × 12½" borders to the sides of the light 12½" center square. Then sew the 1½" × 14½" borders to the top and bottom. The quilt center should measure 14½" square, including seam allowances.

2. Sew the black 4" × 14½" strips to the sides of the quilt center and then sew the black 4" × 21½" strips to the top and bottom. The quilt top should measure 21½" square, including seam allowances.

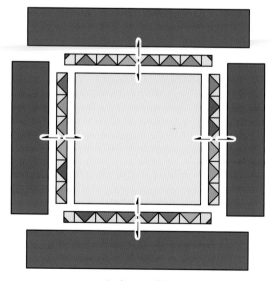

Quilt assembly

FINISHING THE QUILT

1. To create the scalloped border, cut a length of freezer paper approximately 22" long. Fold the freezer paper in half with shiny sides together so that it's 11" long. Place the fold along the dashed line of the scallop pattern on page 12 and trace. Cut out the pattern along the traced line to make a template. The template should measure approximately 3" × 20½".

2. Using a dry iron, press the template onto the black outer border, aligning the straight edge with the seam of the border. Trace around the template with a chalk pencil. It's very important to trace the scalloped border onto the quilt top *before* quilting, but do not cut the scallop border until

after quilting. The traced scallop will serve as a guide for quilting and will be your cutting line after quilting is complete. Reposition the template and trace around it on all four sides of the quilt top.

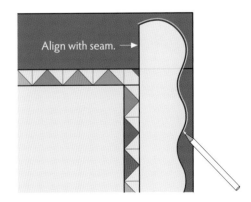

Align with seam.

3. Make, sign, and date a label and attach to the quilt backing, if desired. For my label technique, see "Adding a Label" on page 76.

4. Layer the quilt top with batting and backing. Quilt by hand or by machine. The quilt shown is machine quilted with a crosshatched feathered wreath design in the center square. A petal design is quilted in the flying-geese units, and a curving leaf design is stitched in the scallop border.

5. When quilting is finished, sew a row of straight stitches ⅛" inside the marked scallop line to stabilize the edge of the scallop and help to prevent stretching. Cut the scalloped edge on the drawn line with scissors.

6. Join the black 2¼"-wide strips to make double-fold bias binding that's 100" long. Sew the binding to the quilt top, easing around the curves. Fold the binding to the back of the quilt and hand sew in place. If you need additional details, go to ShopMartingale.com/HowToQuilt for free downloadable information.

ADDING THE YO-YOS

1. Trace the circle pattern on page 12 onto template plastic and cut it out on the drawn line.

2. Trace the circle template onto the wrong side of a scrap of dark fabric. Cut the circle on the drawn line.

3. Thread a needle with a single strand of quilting thread or a double strand of regular sewing thread and knot the end.

4. Fold the raw edge of the circle over to the wrong side approximately ¼". Begin stitching by bringing the needle up under the fold, burying the knot within the fold. Sew a running stitch through the two layers of fabric, folding the fabric over as you go. Stitch all the way around until you reach the starting point. Don't cut the thread!

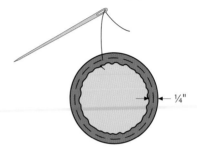

5. Gently pull the thread to gather the edges of the yo-yo. You may need to flatten and shape the gathers to make sure they are in the center. Insert the needle inside and under the gathered edge and through to the back. Make a knot and clip the thread. The completed yo-yo should be approximately 1¼" in diameter. Make 64 yo-yos.

Make 64 yo-yos.

Yo-Yo Details

If the opening in the center of the yo-yo is too large, try taking longer stitches. The larger the stitch length, the tighter the gathers will be in the center, resulting in a smaller opening. Smaller stitches create more gathers, and the opening will be larger because of this.

6. Arrange the yo-yos on your work surface in eight rows of eight yo-yos each until you're pleased with the layout. Using a double strand of regular sewing thread, hand stitch the yo-yos to each other, taking three or four tack stitches at the 3, 6, 9 and 12 o'clock positions. Knot the thread on the wrong side of the yo-yo after stitching each position.

7. Position the stitched yo-yos on top of the quilt. Add a dot of fabric glue under the center of the yo-yos around the outer edge and press them into place. Allow the glue to dry for about an hour. Hand sew tacking stitches on the outer edges only. (I left the center yo-yos unstitched.)

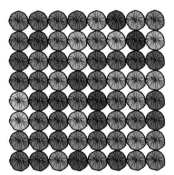

Join yo-yos with tack stitches.

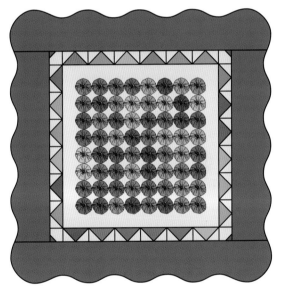

Appliqué placement

Easing to Fit

The yo-yo center will have some spring and give to it. After placing the sewn group on the center of the quilt, ease or stretch it a bit as needed until it fits perfectly in the center of the quilt.

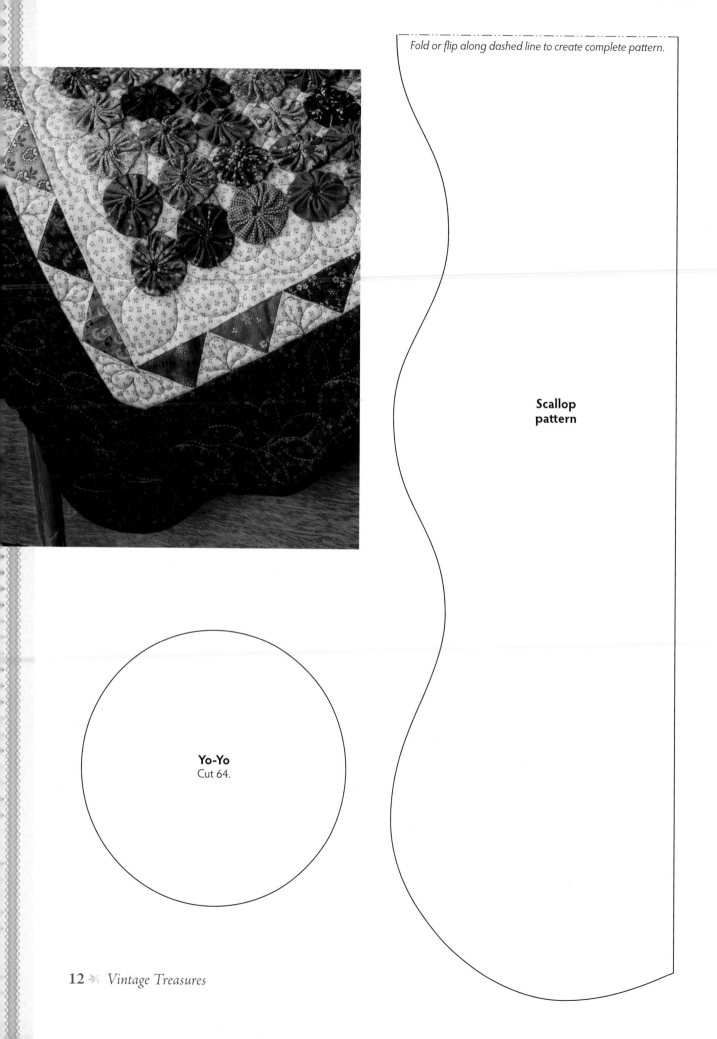

Fold or flip along dashed line to create complete pattern.

Scallop pattern

Yo-Yo
Cut 64.

Olde Postage

Right at home on a tabletop, Olde Postage is reminiscent of a game board, and it would please the heart of every nineteenth-century quiltmaker for its use of scraps. Doesn't frugality look wonderful? For extra fun, swap squares with friends and make a charm quilt with no two fabrics the same.

QUILT SIZE: 18½" × 18½"

LARGE SQUARE SIZE: 1" × 1" | SMALL SQUARE SIZE: ½" × ½"

MATERIALS

Yardage is based on 42"-wide fabric; fat quarters measure 18" × 21".

½ yard *total* of assorted light prints for squares

½ yard *total* of assorted medium and dark prints
for squares (referred to collectively as "dark")

1 fat quarter of red stripe for inner border

¼ yard of blue print for binding

⅔ yard of fabric for backing

23" × 23" piece of batting

CUTTING

From the assorted light prints, cut:
128 squares, 1" × 1"
112 squares, 1½" × 1½"

From the assorted dark prints, cut:
128 squares, 1" × 1"
112 squares, 1½" × 1½"

Continued on page 15

Continued from page 13

From the red stripe, cut on *the lengthwise grain:**

4 strips, 1½" × 18"

From the blue print, cut:

3 strips, 2" × 42"

*For mitered corners, be sure that you cut each 1½" strip from the same part of the stripe so that the stripe will match at the mitered corners.

MAKING THE QUILT CENTER

Press all seam allowances as indicated by the arrows.

1. Sew light and dark 1" squares into pairs to make 128 two-patch units that measure 1" × 1½", including seam allowances.

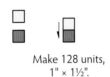

Make 128 units,
1" × 1½".

2. Sew eight two-patch units into a row, sewing light squares to dark squares. The row should measure 1" × 8½", including seam allowances. Make 16 rows. Sew the rows together, alternating dark and light squares to create the checkerboard pattern. The quilt center should measure 8½" square, including seam allowances.

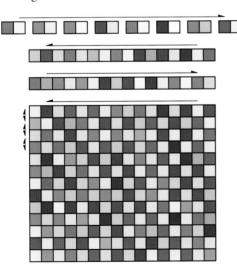

Make 1 quilt center,
8½" × 8½".

Perfect Imperfection

Sewing with tiny pieces like these means accuracy is important. I began by sewing light and dark squares into two-patches and measuring each and every one to be sure they were accurate. Then I pieced the rows together and measured again. When so many squares and seams are involved, sometimes they don't stay perfectly accurate. Just do your best. Our quilting ancestors would think that this approach to quiltmaking is perfectly imperfect!

3. The red border has mitered corners in the quilt shown. To do this, center and sew the red stripe 1½" × 18" borders to the sides, top, and bottom of the quilt center. Start and stop sewing ¼" from the beginning and end and backstitch to secure the stitches. Press the seam allowances toward the border strips.

4. Fold the quilt diagonally with right sides together, aligning the raw edges of two adjacent border strips. Pin the borders together.

OPPOSITE: Designed, pieced, and hand quilted by Pam Buda

5. Place a long acrylic ruler even with the folded edge of the quilt and align the 45° line of the ruler with the border stitching line. With a pencil, draw a line from the point where the ¼" seamline begins to the raw edge of the border strip. Pin along this line to hold the two borders in place. Lift one border strip and check to make sure the position of the miter is correct. Adjust the pins if it's not.

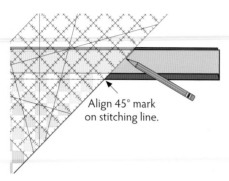

Align 45° mark on stitching line.

Draw a line from the seam intersection to outer edge of borders.

6. Beginning at the end of the border seam, stitch on the pencil line to the edge of the border. Open the borders to check that the stripe matches and the border lays flat. If the mitered corner is sewn correctly, trim the extra border length, leaving a ¼" seam allowance. Press the seam allowances open. Repeat on each corner of the quilt.

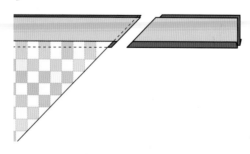

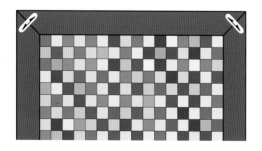

MAKING THE PIECED BORDER

1. Referring to the quilt assembly diagram on page 17, arrange 20 assorted light and 20 assorted dark 1½" squares in 10 rows of four squares each, alternating light and dark to create a checkerboard. Sew the squares into rows and then sew the rows together to make a side border that measures 4½" × 10½", including seam allowances. Make two side borders.

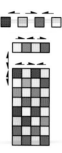

Make 2 side borders,
4½" × 10½".

2. Arrange 36 assorted light and 36 assorted dark 1½" squares in four rows of 18 squares each, alternating the light and dark squares to create a checkerboard. Sew the squares into rows and then sew the rows together to make a border that measures 4½" × 18½", including seam allowances. Make two borders for the top and bottom.

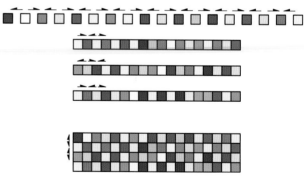

Make 2 top/bottom borders,
4½" × 18½".

3. Sew the side borders to the quilt center and then add the top and bottom borders.

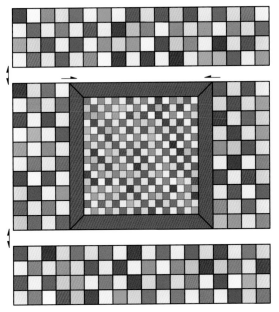

Quilt assembly

FINISHING THE QUILT

1. Make, sign, and date a label and attach to the quilt backing, if desired. For my label technique, see "Adding a Label" on page 76.

2. Layer the quilt top with batting and backing. Quilt by hand or by machine. I hand quilted straight, diagonal lines in one direction through the light squares in the quilt center and straight, diagonal lines in the opposite direction through the dark squares in the quilt center. I hand quilted diagonal lines in both directions through the light squares in the borders.

3. Trim the excess batting and backing. Use the blue 2"-wide strips to make single-fold binding (page 77) and sew the binding to the quilt. If you need additional details, go to ShopMartingale.com for free downloadable information.

Seneca Falls

Lucretia Mott and Elizabeth Cady Stanton met at the World Anti-Slavery Convention in 1840 and began sharing their concerns over the unfair treatment of women in America. Their first convention, held at Seneca Falls, New York, in 1848, is recognized as the first step in the women's rights movement. This quilt honors our foremothers and is dedicated to all women who worked for women's voting rights.

QUILT SIZE: 25¾" × 31½" | **BLOCK SIZE: 2" × 2"**

MATERIALS

Yardage is based on 42"-wide fabric.

⅞ yard of light print for blocks, setting squares, and setting triangles

9 rectangles, 5" × 8", of assorted red prints for Pinwheel blocks

9 rectangles, 5" × 10", of assorted blue prints for Four Patch blocks

½ yard of blue print for border

⅓ yard of red print for binding

1 yard of fabric for backing

30" × 36" piece of batting

CUTTING

From the light print, cut:

1 strip, 4⅛" × 42; crosscut into:

    7 squares, 4⅛" × 4⅛"; cut into quarters diagonally to make 28 triangles

    2 squares, 2⅜" × 2⅜"; cut in half diagonally to make 4 triangles

3 strips, 2½" × 42"; crosscut into 48 squares, 2½" × 2½"

3 strips, 2" × 42"; crosscut into 54 squares, 2" × 2"

4 strips, 1½" × 42"; crosscut into 18 strips, 1½" × 8"

From *each* of the red prints, cut:

6 squares, 2" × 2" (54 total)

From *each* of the blue prints, cut:

2 strips, 1½" × 8" (18 total)

From the blue print for border, cut:

4 strips, 3¼" × 42"; crosscut into 4 strips, 3¼" × 25½"

From the red print for binding, cut:

4 strips, 2¼" × 42"

measuring 2½" square, including seam allowances. Make a total of 27 blocks, three each of the nine different red prints.

Make 27 blocks,
2½" × 2½".

Make Do!

If you'd like to replicate my make-do look, replace four of the blue Four Patch blocks with black blocks. Cut eight 1½" squares from assorted black prints and sew them together with eight light 1½" squares to make four blocks. Make just 32 blue blocks. Place the black blocks randomly in the quilt layout, or look closely at the photograph on page 18 to place them where I did.

FOUR PATCH BLOCKS

1. Sew light and blue 1½" × 8" strips together in pairs to make 18 strip sets. Crosscut 72 segments, 1½" wide.

Make 18 strip sets, 2½" × 8".
Cut 72 segments, 1½" × 2½".

2. Sew two matching or different segments into a Four Patch block. Make a total of 36 blocks measuring 2½" square, including seam allowances.

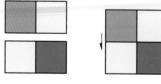

Make 36 blocks,
2½" × 2½".

PINWHEEL BLOCKS

Press all seam allowances as indicated by the arrows.

1. Draw a diagonal line from corner to corner on the wrong side of two light 2" squares. Place each marked square on a red 2" square, right sides together. Sew ¼" from each side of the drawn lines. Cut the units apart on the marked lines and press to make a total of four half-square-triangle units. Trim to 1½" square.

1½"

1½"

Make 4 units.

2. Lay out the half-square-triangle units, rotating them to form a pinwheel. Sew the units into rows. Join the rows to make a Pinwheel block

PIECING THE QUILT CENTER

I used one each of the nine different red print Pinwheels in each of the three columns.

1. Arrange the Four Patch blocks, Pinwheel blocks, light 2½" setting squares, light 4⅛" setting triangles, and light 2⅜" corner triangles in diagonal rows as shown in the quilt assembly

diagram below. Sew the units into rows and then sew the rows together. The quilt center should measure approximately 19¾" × 25½", including seam allowances.

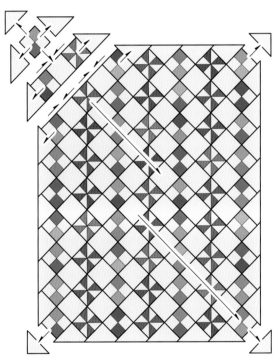

Quilt assembly

2. Measure the length of the quilt through the center and cut two of the blue 3¼" × 42" strips to that measurement. Sew these strips to the sides of the quilt. Press seam allowances toward the border.

3. Measure the width of the quilt through the center, including the blue borders just added. Cut two strips to that measurement from the remaining blue 3¼" × 42" strips. Sew the strips to the top and bottom of the quilt. The quilt top should measure approximately 25¾" × 31½".

FINISHING THE QUILT

1. Make, sign, and date a label and attach to the quilt backing, if desired. For my label technique, see "Adding a Label" on page 76.

2. Layer the quilt top with batting and backing. Quilt by hand or by machine. My quilt is machine quilted with ovals in the Four Patch blocks, triangles in the Pinwheel blocks, and curlicues in the setting squares and triangles. A loose feather design is quilted in the blue border.

3. Trim the excess batting and backing. Use the red 2¼"-wide strips to make double-fold binding and sew the binding to the quilt. If you need additional details, go to ShopMartingale.com for free downloadable information.

Crossroads

There's something about a two-color quilt that elicits warm feelings of tradition.
Our quilting ancestors loved them, and that love has persisted through generations.
Choose a lively, nondirectional print for the background and binding, then smaller
prints for the half-square triangles. Which two colors you choose doesn't matter.
Any direction you go, you're sure to enjoy Crossroads!

QUILT SIZE: 26½" × 26½" | **BLOCK SIZE: 5" × 5"**

MATERIALS

Yardage is based on 42"-wide fabric.

9 rectangles, 6" × 15", of assorted light prints for blocks
9 rectangles, 5" × 9", of assorted red prints for blocks
1 yard of red print for blocks, borders, and binding
¼ yard of dark red print for middle border
⅞ yard of fabric for backing
31" × 31" piece of batting

CUTTING

From *each* of the assorted light prints, cut:

1 square, 4⅞" × 4⅞"; cut in half diagonally to make
    2 triangles (18 total; 6 are extra)
8 squares, 1⅞" × 1⅞" (72 total)

From *each* of the assorted red prints, cut:

8 squares, 1⅞" × 1⅞" (72 total)

From the red print, cut:

2 strips, 4⅞" × 42"; crosscut into 10 squares,
    4⅞" × 4⅞". Cut in half diagonally to make
    20 triangles.
3 strips, 2¼" × 42"
4 strips, 2" × 42"; crosscut into:
    2 strips, 2" × 23½"
    2 strips, 2" × 26½"
4 strips, 1¼" × 42"; crosscut into:*
    2 strips, 1¼" × 20½"
    2 strips, 1¼" × 22"

**Note that 3 strips may be enough if your fabric
is at least 42" wide after removing selvages.*

Continued on page 24

OPPOSITE: Designed by Pam Buda
Pieced by Debbie McClarence
Quilted by Ronda Dranter

Continued from page 23

From the dark red print, cut:
4 strips, 1¼" × 42"; crosscut into:
    2 strips, 1¼" × 22"
    2 strips, 1¼" × 23½"

CROSSROADS BLOCKS

Press all seam allowances as indicated by the arrows.

1. Draw a diagonal line from corner to corner on the wrong side of 40 assorted light 1⅞" squares. Place a marked square on an assorted red 1⅞" square, right sides together. Sew ¼" from each side of the drawn line. Cut the unit apart on the marked line and press to make two half-square-triangle units measuring 1½" square, including seam allowances. Make a total of 80 units.

Make 80 units,
1½" × 1½".

2. Cut the remaining 32 light and 32 red 1⅞" squares in half diagonally to make 64 triangles of each.

3. Choose five of the assorted half-square-triangle units, four light 1⅞" triangles, and four red 1⅞" triangles. Arrange and sew the units and triangles together in rows as shown. Sew the rows together.

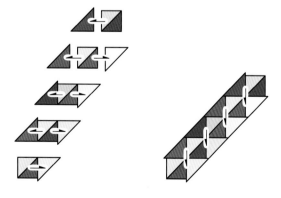

4. Sew light and red 4⅞" triangles to the step 3 units as shown to complete 12 blocks that measure 5½" square, including seam allowances.

Make 12 blocks,
5½" × 5½".

5. Repeat steps 3 and 4 using two red print 4⅞" triangles to make four blocks with red triangles.

Make 4 blocks,
5½" × 5½".

ASSEMBLING THE QUILT

1. Arrange and sew the blocks in four rows of four blocks each as shown, using the blocks with two red triangles in the corners. Sew the rows together to make the quilt center, which should measure 20½" square, including seam allowances.

Quilt assembly

2. Sew the red 1¼" × 20½" borders to the sides of the quilt. Then sew the red 1¼" × 22" borders to the top and bottom. The quilt should measure 22" square, including seam allowances.

3. Sew the dark red 1¼" × 22" borders to the sides of the quilt and the dark red 1¼" × 23½" strips to the top and bottom. The quilt should measure 23½" square, including seam allowances.

4. Sew the red 2" × 23½" border strips to the sides of the quilt and the 2" × 26½" strips to the top and bottom. The quilt should measure 26½" square.

Adding borders

FINISHING THE QUILT

1. Make a label and attach it to the quilt backing, if desired. See "Adding a Label" on page 76.

2. Layer the quilt top with batting and backing. Quilt by hand or by machine. My quilt is machine quilted with curves, swirls, and petals. The inner and middle borders are quilted in the ditch.

3. Trim the excess batting and backing. Use the red 2¼"-wide strips to make double-fold binding and sew the binding to the quilt. If you need additional details, go to ShopMartingale.com for free downloadable information.

Windy Hill Farm

The Preemption Act of 1841 permitted squatters living on government land to acquire up to 160 acres at a low price. Word spread to eastern residents and across the oceans, and the promise of land became a primary reason for coming to America. Windy Hill Farm is dedicated to the pioneer families who lived on homesteads.

QUILT SIZE: 34½" × 42½"

NINE PATCH BLOCK: 6" × 6" | **PINWHEEL BLOCK: 2" × 2"**

MATERIALS

Yardage is based on 42"-wide fabric.

20 squares, 10" × 10", of assorted light prints for Nine Patch blocks

20 squares, 6" × 6", of assorted blue prints for Nine Patch blocks

¼ yard of light print for Pinwheel blocks

¼ yard of black print for Pinwheel blocks

⅞ yard of pink print for sashing

½ yard of blue print for binding

1½ yards of fabric for backing

40" × 48" piece of batting

CUTTING

From *each* of the light print 10" squares, cut:
5 squares, 2½" × 2½" (100 total)

From *each* of the blue print 6" squares, cut:
4 squares, 2½" × 2½" (80 total)

From the light print, cut:
3 strips, 2" × 42"; crosscut 60 squares, 2" × 2"

From the black print, cut:
3 strips, 2" × 42"; crosscut 60 squares, 2" × 2"

From the pink print, cut:
4 strips, 6½" × 42"; crosscut 49 rectangles, 6½" × 2½"

From the blue print, cut:
5 strips, 2¼" × 42"

OPPOSITE: Designed by Pam Buda
Pieced by Pat Creehan
Quilted by Ronda Dranter

Make Do!

I love adding the vintage look of an occasional mismatched piece in my quilts. Several of the blocks in this quilt include make-do fabrics that don't quite match. I feel this adds a lot of interest to the blocks and replicates what our quilting ancestors so often had to do in their quilts. Add make-dos of your own, or keep the blocks orderly. Either way, the quilt will shine.

If you'd like to replicate my make-do look, cut several assorted 2½" squares of both light and blue fabrics for the Nine Patch blocks. How many is up to you. Study the photograph on page 29 to replicate the placement of my make-do fabric substitutions, or insert them in your quilt wherever desired. Then enjoy the charmingly improvised sparkle of your quilt!

NINE PATCH BLOCKS

Press all seam allowances as indicated by the arrows.

Arrange and sew five matching light and four matching blue 2½" squares into three rows as shown, alternating colors. Sew the rows together to make a Nine Patch block measuring 6½" square, including seam allowances. Make a total of 20 Nine Patch blocks.

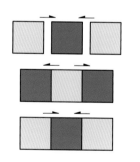

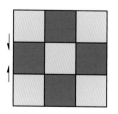

Make 20 blocks,
6½" × 6½".

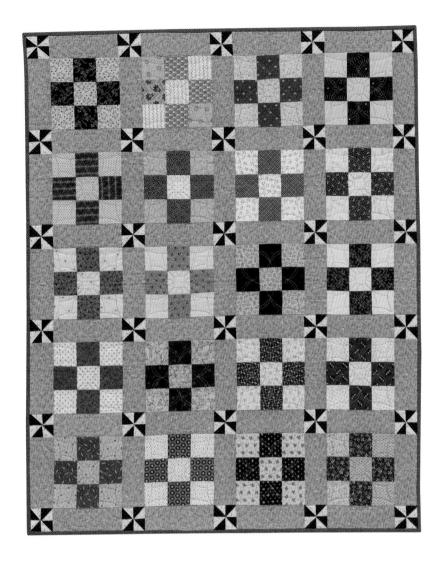

PINWHEEL BLOCKS

1. Draw a diagonal line from corner to corner on the wrong side of the light 2" squares. Place a marked square on each black 2" square, right sides together. Sew ¼" from each side of the drawn lines. Cut apart on the marked lines and press to make 120 half-square-triangle units. Trim the units to 1½" square.

Make 120 units.

2. Lay out four half-square-triangle units in two rows, rotating them to form a pinwheel as shown. Sew the units into rows. Join the rows to make a Pinwheel block that measures 2½" square, including seam allowances. Make a total of 30 Pinwheel blocks.

Make 30 blocks,
2½" × 2½".

ASSEMBLING AND FINISHING THE QUILT

1. Arrange the Nine Patch blocks, the Pinwheel blocks, and the pink 2½" × 6½" sashing strips in rows as shown in the quilt assembly diagram below. Join the pieces in each row, then sew the rows together. The quilt top should measure 34½" × 42½".

2. Make, sign, and date a label and attach to the quilt backing, if desired. For my label technique, see "Adding a Label" on page 76.

3. Layer the quilt top with batting and backing. Quilt by hand or by machine. My quilt is machine quilted with point-to-point curves in the Pinwheels. A curved floral design is quilted in the Nine Patch blocks and sashing.

4. Trim the excess batting and backing. Use the blue 2¼"-wide strips to make double-fold binding and sew the binding to the quilt. If you need additional details, go to ShopMartingale.com for free downloadable information.

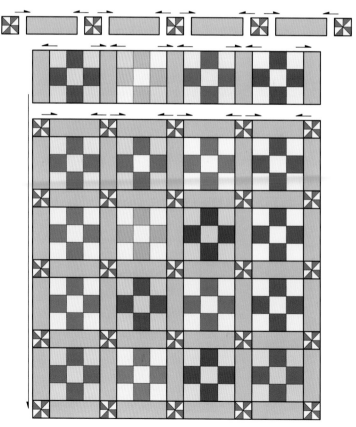

Quilt assembly

A Light in the Window

Candles and oil lamps were the main source of light for homes until the invention of the light bulb in 1879. It's easy to imagine a prairie woman sitting in her chair, stitching a sampler or piecing a quilt by the light of a candle she likely made herself. How brightly a light in the window must have shown against the dark night sky of the prairie!

QUILT SIZE: 23" × 27¼" | BLOCK SIZE: 3" × 3"

MATERIALS

Yardage is based on 42"-wide fabric.

20 scraps, 4" × 8", of assorted light prints for blocks

10 scraps, 4" × 8", of assorted blue prints for blocks

10 scraps, 4" × 8", of assorted green prints for blocks

⅜ yard of light green print for setting squares and
  inner border

⅝ yard of navy print for setting triangles and
  outer border

¼ yard of green print for binding

⅞ yard of fabric for backing

27" × 32" piece of batting

CUTTING

From *each* of the assorted light prints, cut:
1 strip, 1" × 7" (20 total)
2 squares, 2" × 2" (40 total)
1 square, 1½" × 1½" (20 total)

From *each* of the assorted blue prints, cut:
1 strip, 1" × 7" (10 total)
2 squares, 2" × 2" (20 total)

From *each* of the assorted green prints, cut:
1 strip, 1" × 7" (10 total)
2 squares, 2" × 2" (20 total)

From the light green print, cut:
2 strips, 3½" × 42"; crosscut into 12 squares,
  3½" × 3½"
3 strips, 1¼" × 42"; crosscut into:
  2 strips, 1¼" × 21¾"
  2 strips, 1¼" × 19"

Continued on page 33

Continued from page 31

From the navy print, cut:

1 strip, 5½" × 42"; crosscut into:

   4 squares, 5½" × 5½"; cut into quarters diagonally
      to make 16 triangles (2 are extra)

   2 squares, 3" × 3"; cut in half diagonally to make
      4 triangles

4 strips, 2½" × 42"; crosscut into:

   2 strips, 2½" × 23¼"

   2 strips, 2½" × 23"

From the green print for binding, cut:

3 strips, 2¼" × 42"

CHURN DASH BLOCKS

Press all seam allowances as indicated by the arrows.

1. For each blue block, choose the following pieces:
A matching set of:

   • 2 light 2" squares

   • 1 light 1" × 7" strip

   • 1 light 1½" square

A matching set of:

   • 2 blue 2" squares

   • 1 blue 1" × 7" strip

Make Do!

*If you'd like to replicate my make-do look,
mix in scrap pieces for a few of the half-square
triangles or block centers. Subtle mismatches
give quilts both a vintage feel and visual depth.*

2. Draw a diagonal line from corner to corner on
the wrong side of each light 2" square. Place each
marked square on a blue 2" square, right sides
together. Sew ¼" from each side of the drawn
lines. Cut the units apart on the marked lines
and press to make four half-square-triangle units.
Trim the units to 1½" square.

Make 4 units.

3. Sew the light and blue 1" × 7" strips together to
create a strip set that measures 1½" × 7", including
seam allowances. Cut four segments, 1½" wide,
from the strip set.

Make 1 strip set, 1½" × 7".
Cut 4 segments, 1½" × 1½".

4. Arrange and sew the four half-square-triangle
units, the four segments, and the light 1½" square
together in three rows. Join the rows and press
to make a Churn Dash block that measures
3½" square, including seam allowances. Make
10 blue blocks. Repeat, swapping green for blue,
to make 10 green blocks.

Make 10 blocks,   Make 10 blocks,
3½" × 3½".   3½" × 3½".

**OPPOSITE: Designed and pieced by Pam Buda
Quilted by Ronda Dranter**

ASSEMBLING THE QUILT

1. Lay out the 20 Churn Dash blocks, light green 3½" setting squares, navy 5½" setting triangles, and navy 3" corner triangles in diagonal rows as shown. Sew the blocks, squares, and triangles into rows. Sew the rows together. The quilt center should measure 17½" × 21¾", including seam allowances.

2. Sew the light green 1¼" × 21¾" border strips to the sides of the quilt center; press. Then sew the light green 1¼" × 19" borders to the top and bottom of the quilt; press. The quilt center should measure 19" × 23¼".

3. Sew the navy 2½" × 23¼" border strips to the sides of the quilt. Sew the navy 2½" × 23" strips to the top and bottom. The quilt top should measure 23" × 27¼".

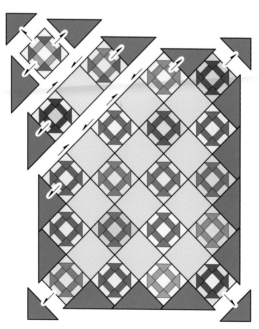

Quilt assembly

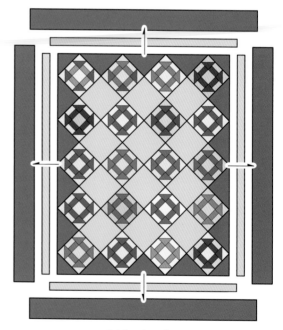

Adding borders

FINISHING THE QUILT

1. Make, sign, and date a label and attach to the quilt backing, if desired. For my label technique, see "Adding a Label" on page 76.

2. Layer the quilt top with batting and backing. Quilt by hand or by machine. My quilt is machine quilted. The Churn Dash blocks are quilted in the ditch and a lovely curved design with loops and petals is quilted in the setting squares and triangles. The light green inner border is quilted in the ditch and a leaf and swirl design enhances the navy outer border.

3. Trim the excess batting and backing. Use the green 2¼"-wide strips to make double-fold binding and sew the binding to the quilt. If you need additional help, go to ShopMartingale.com for free downloadable information.

Hallow's Eve

I see pumpkins with jack-o'-lantern faces in these blocks, and they make me smile every time I look at them. Enjoy making this quilt with your favorite black and orange fabric for the perfect spooky vignette. Or, if you prefer, stretch the palette with soft apricot, cheery marigold, and deep amber to make every block different.

QUILT SIZE: 13" × 13" | **BLOCK SIZE: 4½ × 4½**

MATERIALS

Yardage is based on 42"-wide fabric.

¼ yard of orange print for blocks, center square, and corner units

½ yard of black print for blocks, sashing, borders, and binding

½ yard of fabric for backing

17" × 17" piece of batting

OPPOSITE: Designed, pieced, and hand quilted by Pam Buda

CUTTING

From the orange print, cut:
1 strip, 2⅜" × 42"; crosscut into:
    16 rectangles, 1¼" × 2⅜"
    6 squares, 1¾" × 1¾"
    1 square 1½" × 1½"
1 strip, 2¼" × 42"; crosscut into:
    10 squares, 2¼" × 2¼"
    10 squares, 1¾" × 1¾"

From the black print, cut:
1 strip, 2¼" × 42"; crosscut into:
    10 squares, 2¼" × 2¼"
    10 squares, 1¾" × 1¾"
2 strips, 2" × 42"
2 strips, 1¾" × 42"; crosscut into:
    4 strips, 1¾" × 10½"
    6 squares, 1¾" × 1¾"
    16 rectangles, 1¾" × 1⅛"
1 strip, 1½" × 42"; crosscut into:
    4 rectangles, 1½" × 5"
    16 squares, 1⅛" × 1⅛"
4 squares, 1¼" × 1¼"

MAKING THE BLOCKS

Press all seam allowances as indicated by the arrows.

1. Draw a diagonal line from corner to corner on the wrong side of the 10 orange 2¼" squares. Place each marked square on a black 2¼" square, right sides together. Sew ¼" from each side of the drawn lines. Cut the units apart on the marked lines and press to make a total of 20 half-square-triangle units. Trim each to measure 1¾" square. Set aside four of the units to be used in the border corners.

Make 20 units.

2. In the same manner, use 16 orange and 16 black 1¾" squares to make a total of 32 half-square-triangle units. Trim each unit to measure 1⅛" square.

Make 32 units.

3. Arrange one 1¾" unit, two 1⅛" units, one black 1⅛" × 1¾" rectangle, and one black 1⅛" square as shown. Sew into rows; press. Join the rows. Make 16 units that are 2⅜" square, including seam allowances.

Make 16 units,
2⅜" × 2⅜".

4. Arrange four units from step 3, four orange 1¼" × 2⅜" rectangles, and one black 1¼" square as shown. Sew into rows; press. Sew the rows together to make a block measuring 5" square, including seam allowances. Make four blocks.

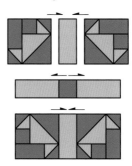

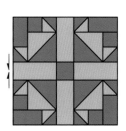

Make 4 blocks,
5" × 5".

Try Hand Quilting

I just recently started hand quilting, and honestly, I'm hooked! This little quilt doesn't require a lot of quilting and is suited to simple straight lines, which makes it a perfect launch point. I also hand quilted Olde Postage on page 13. As they say, practice makes perfect!

ASSEMBLING THE QUILT

1. Arrange the four blocks, the four black 1½" × 5" sashing strips, and the orange 1½" square in rows as shown in the quilt assembly diagram below. Sew into rows; sew the rows together. The quilt center should measure 10½" square, including seam allowances.

2. Sew a black 1¾" × 10½" border to each side of the quilt center. Sew a 1¾" half-square triangle to each end of the remaining black borders. Sew these to the top and bottom of the quilt and press. The quilt should measure 13" square.

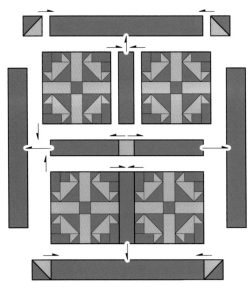

Quilt assembly

FINISHING THE QUILT

1. Make, sign, and date a label and attach to the quilt backing, if desired. For my label technique, see "Adding a Label" on page 76.

2. Layer the quilt top with batting and backing. Quilt by hand or by machine. I quilted by hand with easy, straight-line quilting stitches in the center of the sashing strips. I echo stitched ¼" from the orange fabric in the blocks and added a simple cable in the borders.

3. Trim the excess batting and backing. Use the black 2"-wide strips to make single-fold binding (page 77) and sew the binding to the quilt.

Colonial Star

Feathered Star quilts are so captivating, yet many of us shy away from making one because they look challenging. This version features everything you love about the classic design but without any set-in seams. You'll love how Colonial Star comes together easily, looks impressive, and adds warmth to any decor.

QUILT SIZE: 18½" × 20½" | **CENTER OHIO STAR BLOCK SIZE: 5⅝" × 5⅝"**

MATERIALS

Yardage is based on 42"-wide fabric.

½ yard of light print for blocks and borders

¾ yard of blue print for blocks, borders, and binding

¾ yard of fabric for backing

23" × 25" piece of batting

CUTTING

From the light print, cut:

1 strip, 5¼" × 42"; crosscut into:

    2 squares, 5¼" × 5¼"; cut into quarters diagonally to make 4 triangles (8 total)

    2 squares, 3⅝" × 3⅝"

    1 square, 2⅜" × 2⅜"

2 strips, 2" × 42"; crosscut into 25 squares, 2" × 2"

2 strips, 1¼" × 42"; crosscut into:

    2 strips, 1¼" × 15"

    2 strips, 1¼" × 15½"

From the blue print, cut:

1 strip, 5¼" × 42"; crosscut into:

    1 square, 5¼" × 5¼"; cut into quarters diagonally to yield 4 triangles

    2 squares, 3⅝" × 3⅝"

    4 squares, 3½" × 3½"

    4 squares, 2⅜" × 2⅜"

5 strips, 2¼" × 42"; crosscut 2 of the strips into:

    2 strips, 2¼" × 17"

    2 strips, 2¼" × 18½"

2 strips, 2" × 42"; crosscut into:

    25 squares, 2" × 2"

    4 squares, 1½" × 1½"

2 strips, 1" × 42"; crosscut into:

    2 strips, 1" × 12½"

    2 strips, 1" × 13½"

OPPOSITE: Designed by Pam Buda
Pieced by Debbie McClarence
Quilted by Ronda Dranter

OHIO STAR BLOCK

Press all seam allowances as indicated by the arrows.

1. Draw a diagonal line from corner to corner on the wrong side of two light 3⅝" squares. Place each marked square on a blue 3⅝" square, right sides together. Sew ¼" from each side of the drawn lines. Cut the units apart and press to make four half-square-triangle units that measure 3¼" square, including seam allowances.

Make 4 units,
3¼" × 3¼".

2. On the wrong side of two of the half-square-triangle units, draw a diagonal line from corner to corner, perpendicular to the seam allowance. Place a marked unit on an unmarked unit, right sides together with lights on opposite sides and seam allowances nesting together.

3. Sew ¼" from each side of the drawn line; cut the unit apart and press. Repeat for the remaining half-square-triangle units to make four quarter-square-triangle units. Trim the units to measure 2⅜". To trim the units accurately, place the ruler on the block so that the center of the block is 1³⁄₁₆" from the top and from the side. This is halfway between 1⅛" and 1¼". Trim the side and top. Rotate the block 180° and align the trimmed edges with the 2⅜" lines on the ruler. Trim the remaining two sides.

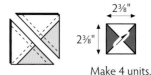

Make 4 units.

4. Arrange and sew the four quarter-square-triangle units, one light 2⅜" square, and four blue 2⅜" squares in three rows as shown. Sew the rows together and press to make one Ohio Star block measuring 6⅛" square, including seam allowances.

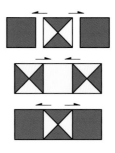 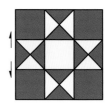

Make 1 block,
6⅛" × 6⅛".

HALF-SQUARE-TRIANGLE UNITS

Draw a diagonal line from corner to corner on the wrong side of 25 light 2" squares. Place each marked square right sides together on a blue 2" square. Sew, cut, and press as in step 1 of "Ohio Star Block" on page 42 to make 50 half-square-triangle units. Trim the units to measure 1½" square.

Make 50 units.

SAWTOOTH CORNER BLOCKS

1. Sew three half-square-triangle units into a row as shown. The row should measure 1½" × 3½". Make a second row with the triangles angled in the opposite direction and add a blue 1½" square to the right side to make a row that measures 1½" × 4½". Make four of each row.

Make 4 rows, 1½" × 3½".

Make 4 rows, 1½" × 4½".

2. Sew one of each row to the right and bottom of a blue 3½" square as shown to make a Sawtooth Corner block measuring 4½" square, including seam allowances. Make four blocks.

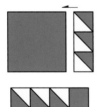

Make 4 blocks, 4½" × 4½".

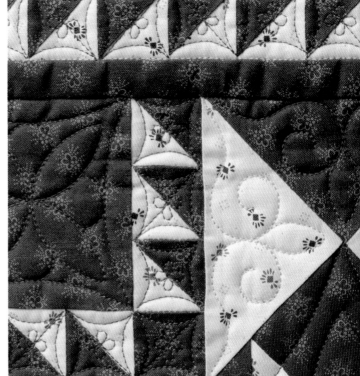

2. Sew two blue 5¼" triangles to a corner unit from step 1. Make two units.

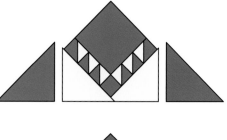

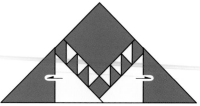

Make 2 units.

3. Sew the units from steps 1 and 2 to the Ohio Star block as shown to make the quilt center. It should measure 12½" square, including seam allowances.

Make 1 block,
12½" × 12½".

ADDING THE BORDERS

1. Sew the blue 1" × 12½" borders to the sides of the quilt center, and then sew the blue 1" × 13½" strips to the top and bottom. The quilt should measure 13½" square, including seam allowances.

2. Sew 13 of the 1½" half-square-triangle units together as shown to make a border measuring 1½" × 13½", including seam allowances. Make two borders.

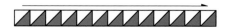

Make 2 borders,
1½" × 13½".

ASSEMBLING THE QUILT CENTER

1. Sew two light 5¼" triangles to adjacent sides of a Sawtooth Corner block as shown. Make four corner units.

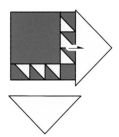

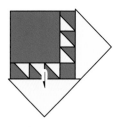

Make 4 corner units.

3. Sew the pieced borders to the top and bottom of the quilt center and press. The quilt center should measure 13½" × 15½", including seam allowances.

4. Sew the light 1¼" × 15½" border strips to the sides of the quilt center, and then sew the light 1¼" × 15" strips to the top and bottom. The quilt should measure 15" × 17", including seam allowances.

5. Sew the blue 2¼" × 17" border strips to the sides of the quilt center, and then sew the blue 2¼" × 18½" strips to the top and bottom. The quilt should measure 18½" × 20½".

FINISHING THE QUILT

1. Make, sign, and date a label and attach to the quilt backing, if desired. For my label technique, see "Adding a Label" on page 76.

2. Layer the quilt top with batting and backing. Quilt by hand or by machine. My quilt is machine quilted with a stylized floral design in the Ohio Star. Fleur-de-lis designs are quilted into the quarter-square triangles. Petals and arcs are stitched to the plain blue corner squares and repeated in the blue outer border. Point-to-point curves are quilted in the half-square-triangle units and a swirl design is stitched in the light print inner border.

3. Trim the excess batting and backing. Use the blue 2¼"-wide strips to make double-fold binding and sew the binding to the quilt. If you need additional details, go to ShopMartingale.com for free downloadable information.

Quilt assembly

Stillwater Creek

In the nineteenth century, little girls began sewing as soon as they could manage a needle, and it wasn't long before they would begin making patchwork quilts for a home they would have in their adult life. After all, a home tastefully embellished with the products of a woman's needle would have an uplifting influence on its inhabitants.

QUILT SIZE: 18½" × 22½" | **BLOCK SIZE: 4½" × 4½"**

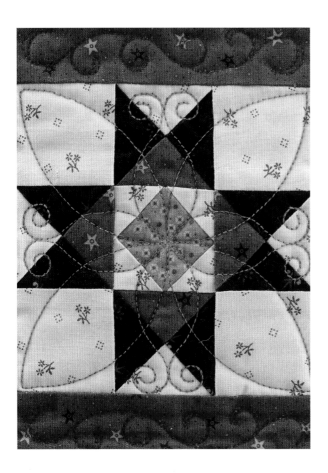

MATERIALS

Yardage is based on 42"-wide fabric.

½ yard of light print for blocks and borders

⅓ yard of red print for blocks, sashing, pieced border, and border corners

⅛ yard of black print for blocks, sashing squares, and pieced border

⅛ yard of gold print for blocks, sashing squares, and pieced border

½ yard of black floral for borders and binding

¾ yard of fabric for backing

23" × 27" piece of batting

**OPPOSITE: Designed by Pam Buda
Pieced by Debbie McClarence
Quilted by Ronda Dranter**

CUTTING

From the light print, cut:

1 strip, 2¾" × 42"; crosscut into:

    4 squares, 2¾" × 2¾"

    16 squares, 1½" × 1½"

1 strip, 2" × 42"; crosscut into 16 squares, 2" × 2"

4 strips, 1½" × 42"; crosscut into:

    2 strips, 1½" × 14½"

    2 strips, 1½" × 12½"

    56 squares, 1½" × 1½"

1 strip, 1¼" × 42"; crosscut into 16 squares, 1¼" × 1¼"

From the red print, cut:

1 strip, 2¾" × 42"; crosscut into:

    4 squares, 2¾" × 2¾"

    4 squares, 2½" × 2½"

1 strip, 2½" × 42"; crosscut into 20 rectangles, 1½" × 2½"

2 strips, 1½" × 42"; crosscut into 12 rectangles, 1½" × 5"

From the black print, cut:

1 strip, 2¾" × 42"; crosscut into:

    8 squares, 2¾" × 2¾"

    2 squares, 2½" × 2½"

    5 squares, 1½" × 1½"

From the gold print, cut:

1 strip, 2" × 42"; crosscut into 4 squares, 2" × 2". Trim the remainder of the strip to 1½" wide, and cut:

    4 rectangles, 1½" × 2½"

    4 squares, 1½" × 1½"

From the black floral, cut:

2 strips, 2½" × 42"; crosscut into:

    2 strips, 2½" × 18½"

    2 strips, 2½" × 14½"

3 strips, 2¼" × 42"

OHIO STAR BLOCKS

Press all seam allowances as indicated by the arrows.

1. Draw a diagonal line from corner to corner on the wrong side of a light and a red 2¾" square. Place each marked square on a black print 2¾" square, right sides together. Sew ¼" from each side of the drawn lines; cut the units apart on the lines and press to make two light/black and two red/black half-square-triangle units that measure 2⅜" square, including seam allowances.

Make 2 units, 2⅜" × 2⅜".

Make 2 units, 2⅜" × 2⅜".

2. On the wrong side of two of the light/black half-square-triangle units, draw a diagonal line from corner to corner, perpendicular to the seam. Align the marked units right sides together with a red/black half-square-triangle unit so that the black prints are facing a red or light triangle and that the seam allowances nest together. Sew ¼" from each side of the drawn lines; cut apart and press to make four hourglass units measuring 2" square, including seam allowances.

Make 4 units, 2" × 2".

3. Repeat steps 1 and 2 to make 16 hourglass units.

4. Referring to "Connector Corners" on page 74, draw a diagonal line from corner to corner on the wrong side of four light 1¼" squares. Place a marked square on the corner of a gold 2" square,

right sides together. Sew on the drawn line; press and trim. Repeat with the remaining three corners to make a square-in-a-square unit measuring 2" square, including seam allowances.

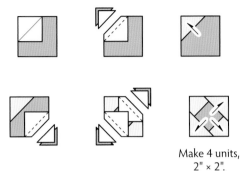

Make 4 units,
2" × 2".

5. Arrange and sew the four hourglass units, the square-in-a-square unit, and four light 2" squares in three rows. Sew the rows together and press to make an Ohio Star block measuring 5" × 5", including seam allowances. Make four blocks.

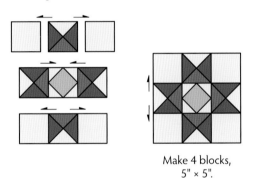

Make 4 blocks,
5" × 5".

BORDER UNITS

1. Draw a diagonal line from corner to corner on the wrong side of two light 1½" squares. Place a marked square on one end of a red 1½" × 2½" rectangle. Stitch on the marked line. Press, making sure the raw edges of the triangle are aligned with the edges of the rectangle. Trim away the excess corner fabric, leaving a ¼" seam allowance. Press the triangle back in place. Place a marked square on the opposite end of the rectangle and repeat to make a flying-geese unit measuring 1½" × 2½", including seam allowances. Make a total of 20 red flying-geese units. Repeat

with light 1½" squares and the gold 1½" × 2½" rectangles to make four gold flying-geese units.

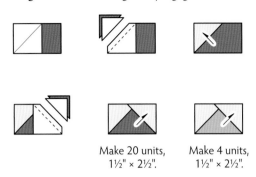

Make 20 units,   Make 4 units,
1½" × 2½".   1½" × 2½".

2. Repeat step 5 of "Ohio Star Blocks" (page 48) to make square-in-a-square units. Make two black print units for the flying-geese borders using light 1½" squares and black 2½" squares. Make four red units for the outer border corners using light 1½" squares and red 2½" squares.

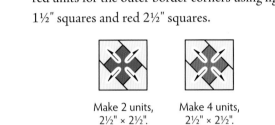

Make 2 units,   Make 4 units,
2½" × 2½".   2½" × 2½".

ASSEMBLING THE QUILT

1. Arrange the four Ohio Star blocks, the red 1½" × 5" sashing strips, five black 1½" squares, and four gold 1½" squares as shown. Sew the pieces into rows. Join the rows and press. The quilt center should measure 12½" square, including seam allowances.

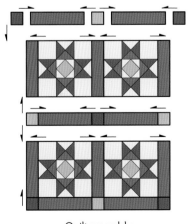

Quilt assembly

end of the black floral 2½" × 14½" border strips and sew them to the top and bottom of the quilt. The quilt should measure 18½" × 22½".

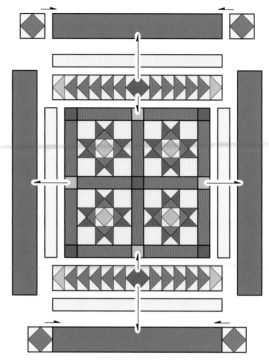

Quilt assembly

2. Sew the light 1½" × 12½" border strips to the sides of the quilt center; press.

3. Sew two gold flying-geese units, 10 red flying-geese units, and a black square-in-a-square unit together as shown to make a pieced border measuring 2½" × 14½", including seam allowances. Make two pieced borders.

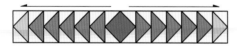

Make 2 borders,
2½" × 14½".

4. Sew the pieced borders to the top and bottom of the quilt; press.

5. Sew the light 1½" × 14½" border strips to the top and bottom of the quilt center; press. The quilt should measure 14½" × 18½", including seam allowances.

6. Sew the two black floral 2½" × 18½" border strips to the sides of the quilt center and press. Sew a red square-in-a-square unit to each

FINISHING THE QUILT

1. Make, sign, and date a label and attach to the quilt backing, if desired. For my label technique, see "Adding a Label" on page 76.

2. Layer the quilt top with batting and backing. Quilt by hand or by machine. My quilt is machine quilted with a floral design in the Ohio Star blocks and a simple curlicue design in the sashing. A petal design is stitched in the flying-geese units and light borders. The square-in-a-square units are quilted in the ditch and a leaf design is quilted in the black floral border.

3. Trim the excess batting and backing. Use the black floral 2¼"-wide strips to make double-fold binding and sew the binding to the quilt. For additional details, go to ShopMartingale.com for free downloadable information.

Emma's Sewing Basket

A woman living on the prairie had a constant companion in the form of her sewing needles. Pins, needles, and scissors were much more than just the tools she used for the many sewing tasks at hand. Patsy Orlofsky writes in her book, Quilts in America, "An old-time quiltmaker used a needle as often, as easily, and casually as we use the telephone; it was her duty, her comfort, her companion, her mode of self-expression."

QUILT SIZE: 35¼" × 35" | **BLOCK SIZE: 4" × 4"**

MATERIALS

Yardage is based on 42"-wide fabric.

23 scraps, 7" × 9", of assorted medium and light prints for blocks (referred to collectively as "light")

11 scraps, 7" × 9", of assorted red prints for blocks

12 scraps, 7" × 9", of assorted brown prints for blocks

1 yard of red print for setting triangles and binding

½ yard of brown print for borders

1¼ yards of fabric for backing

41" × 42" piece of batting

CUTTING

From *each* of the 23 assorted light prints, cut:

4 squares, 2" × 2" (92 total)

4 rectangles, 1½" × 2½" (92 total)

From the assorted red prints, cut:

11 *matching sets* of:

    2 squares, 2" × 2" (22 total)

    8 squares, 1½" × 1½" (88 total)

12 *matching sets* of 2 squares, 2" × 2" (24 total)

From the assorted brown prints, cut:

12 *matching sets* of:

    2 squares, 2" × 2" (24 total)

    8 squares, 1½" × 1½" (96 total)

11 *matching sets* of 2 squares, 2" × 2" (22 total)

From the red print, cut:

2 strips, 7¼" × 42"; crosscut into 10 squares,

    7¼" × 7¼". Cut into quarters diagonally to make

    40 A triangles.

1 strip, 7" × 42"; crosscut into:

    2 squares, 7" × 7"; cut in half diagonally to make

        4 B triangles

    6 squares, 4" × 4"; cut in half diagonally to make

        12 C triangles

4 strips, 2¼" × 42"

From the brown print, cut:

4 strips, 3½" × 42"; crosscut into:

    2 strips, 3½" × 35¼"

    2 strips, 3½" × 29"

OPPOSITE: Designed by Pam Buda
Pieced by Debbie McClarence
Quilted by Ronda Dranter

MAKING THE BLOCKS

Press all seam allowances as indicated by the arrows. The quilt shown includes 12 brown blocks with red pinwheels and 11 red blocks with brown pinwheels.

1. To make a block with a red pinwheel, choose the following pieces.

   A matching set of:

   - 4 light 2" squares
   - 4 light 1½" × 2½" rectangles

   2 matching red 2" squares

   A matching set of:

   - 2 brown 2" squares
   - 8 brown 1½" squares

2. Draw a diagonal line from corner to corner on the wrong side of the four light 2" squares. Place the marked squares on two red and two brown 2" squares, right sides together. Sew ¼" from each side of the drawn lines. Cut the units apart on the marked lines and press to make four red and four brown half-square-triangle units. Trim each unit to 1½" square.

Make 4 of each unit.

3. Arrange and sew the red half-square-triangle units into two rows, rotating them as shown to form a pinwheel. Sew the rows together to make a pinwheel unit that measures 2½" square, including seam allowances.

Make 1 unit,
2½" × 2½".

4. Referring to "Connector Corners" on page 74, draw a diagonal line from corner to corner on the wrong side of the brown 1½" squares. Place a marked square on one end of a light 1½" × 2½" rectangle. Stitch on the line. Press, aligning the edges of the triangle with the rectangle. Trim the excess corner fabric, leaving a ¼" seam allowance. Repeat on the other end of the rectangle to make a brown flying-geese unit measuring 1½" × 2½", including seam allowances. Make four units.

Make 4 units,
1½" × 2½".

5. Arrange and sew the units from steps 3 and 4 with the four brown 1½" units from step 2 in three rows as shown. Sew the rows together to complete a block that measures 4½" square, including seam allowances. Make 12 blocks total.

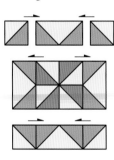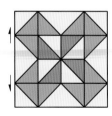

Make 12 blocks,
4½" × 4½".

6. Repeat steps 1–5, swapping the red and brown prints, to make 11 blocks with brown pinwheels.

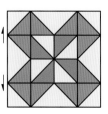

Make 11 blocks,
4½" × 4½".

ASSEMBLING THE QUILT

1. Arrange the blocks and setting triangles in five columns. Columns 1, 3, and 5 each have five blocks, four C triangles, and eight A triangles. Columns 2 and 4 each have four blocks, two B triangles, and eight A triangles. Sew the blocks together and press. The setting triangles are cut slightly oversized. Trim each column to measure 6¼" × 29".

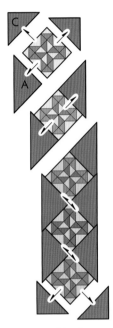 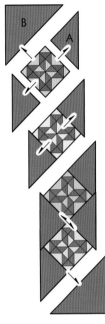

Make 3 odd columns,
6¼" × 29".

Make 2 even columns,
6¼" × 29".

2. Sew the columns together; press. The quilt center should measure 29¼" × 29", including seam allowances.

3. Sew the brown 3½" × 29" border strips to the sides of the quilt center; press. Then sew the brown 3½" × 35¼" strips to the top and bottom. The quilt should measure 35¼" × 35".

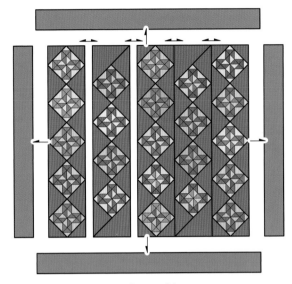

Quilt assembly

FINISHING THE QUILT

1. Make, sign, and date a label and attach to the quilt backing, if desired. For my label technique, see "Adding a Label" on page 76.

2. Layer the quilt top with batting and backing. Quilt by hand or by machine. My quilt is machine quilted. The blocks are quilted in the ditch with point-to-point curves in the light print. A feather design is quilted in the red background and in the brown border.

3. Trim the excess batting and backing. Use the red 2¼"-wide strips to make double-fold binding and sew the binding to the quilt. If you need additional details, go to ShopMartingale.com for free downloadable information.

Conestoga Stitches

Made from my Conestoga Crossing fabric collection, this quilt honors the thousands of men, women, and children who braved the Oregon-California Trail to settle the West. It's unlikely that whole quilts were pieced during the journey, but I don't doubt that women kept scraps in their pockets to enjoy a few moments of sewing.

QUILT SIZE: 24½" × 24½"

OHIO STAR BLOCK SIZE: 4½" × 4½" | **NINE PATCH AND PINWHEEL BLOCK SIZE: 1½" × 1½"**

MATERIALS

Yardage is based on 42"-wide fabric.

1 scrap, 4" × 4", of green print #1 for Ohio Star block

1 scrap, 3" × 3", of gold print #1 for Ohio Star block

1 scrap, 4" × 4", of light print #1 for Ohio Star block

¼ yard of light print #2 for Ohio Star block and setting blocks

⅛ yard of blue print for Ohio Star block, Pinwheel blocks, border 2, and border 4

⅓ yard of black print #1 for Ohio Star block, setting blocks, border 1, and border 2

¼ yard of red print #1 for Nine Patch blocks and border 2

⅛ yard of light print #3 for Nine Patch blocks

1 scrap, 4" × 8", of green print #2 for Pinwheel blocks

1 scrap, 4" × 6", of gold print #2 for setting blocks

¼ yard of light print #4 for border 2

1 scrap, 4" × 4", of red print #2 for border 2

⅛ yard of gold print #3 for border 3

¼ yard of red print #3 for border 4

⅞ yard of black print #2 for border 4, border 5, and binding

⅞ yard of fabric for backing

29" × 29" piece of batting

OPPOSITE: Designed and pieced by Pam Buda
Quilted by Ronda Dranter

CUTTING

Starch your fabrics before cutting. You'll have better control over the small pieces needed for this quilt—especially when using triangles with bias edges. See "Starching Fabrics" on page 73 for instructions.

From green print #1, cut:
4 squares, 1¼" × 1¼"

From gold print #1, cut:
1 square, 2" × 2"

From light print #1, cut:
1 square, 3" × 3"; cut into quarters diagonally
 to make 4 triangles

From light print #2, cut:
1 strip, 3" × 42"; crosscut into:
 2 squares, 3" × 3"; cut into quarters diagonally
  to make 8 triangles
 10 squares, 2½" × 2½"
1 strip, 1¾" × 42"; crosscut into 16 squares,
 1¾" × 1¾"

From the blue print, cut:
1 strip, 3" × 42"; crosscut into:
 2 squares, 3" × 3"; cut into quarters diagonally
  to make 8 triangles
 2 squares, 2½" × 2½"
 14 squares, 1¾" × 1¾"

From black print #1, cut:
1 strip, 3" × 42"; crosscut into:
 1 square, 3" × 3"; cut into quarters diagonally
  to make 4 triangles
 8 squares, 2½" × 2½"
2 squares, 2½" × 2½"; cut in half diagonally to make
 4 triangles
2 strips, 1⅞" × 42"; crosscut into 24 squares,
 1⅞" × 1⅞". Cut in half diagonally to make
 48 triangles.
2 strips, 1¼" × 42; crosscut into:
 2 strips, 1¼" × 12½"
 2 strips, 1¼" × 11"

From red print #1, cut:
1 strip, 1¾" × 42"; crosscut into 6 squares, 1¾" × 1¾"
2 strips, 1" × 42"; crosscut into:
 2 strips, 1" × 26"
 1 strip, 1" × 14"

From light print #3, cut:
2 strips, 1" × 42"; crosscut into:
 1 strip, 1" × 26"
 2 strips, 1" × 14"

From green print #2, cut:
8 squares, 1¾" × 1¾"

From gold print #2, cut:
2 squares, 2½" × 2½"

From light print #4, cut:
1 strip, 2¼" × 42"; crosscut into 12 squares,
 2¼" × 2¼". Cut into quarters diagonally
 to make 48 triangles.
1 strip, 1¾" × 42"; crosscut into 12 squares,
 1¾" × 1¾"

From red print #2, cut:
4 squares, 1½" × 1½"

From gold print #3, cut:
2 strips, 1" × 42"; crosscut into:
 2 strips, 1" × 15½"
 2 strips, 1" × 14½"

From red print #3, cut:
4 strips, 1¼" × 42"; crosscut into 80 rectangles,
 1¼" × 2"

From black print #2, cut:
3 strips, 3½" × 42"; crosscut into:
 2 strips, 3½" × 24½"
 2 strips, 3½" × 18½"
 2 squares, 2½" × 2½"
3 strips, 2¼" × 42"
5 strips, 1¼" × 42"; crosscut into 160 squares,
 1¼" × 1¼"

OHIO STAR BLOCK

Press all seam allowances as indicated by the arrows.

1. Referring to "Connector Corners" on page 74, draw a diagonal line from corner to corner on the wrong side of the four 1¼" green #1 squares. Place a marked square on the corner of a 2" gold #1 square, right sides together. Sew on the drawn line, press, and trim the seam allowances to ¼". Repeat with the remaining three corners to make a square-in-a-square unit that measures 2" square, including seam allowances.

Make 1 unit,
2" × 2".

2. Using 3" light #1 and light #2 triangles, sew each triangle to a blue 3" triangle as shown. Sew the units together to make a star-point unit. Trim the unit to measure 2" square placing the 1" lines of your ruler on the center of the unit when trimming. Make four units.

Make 4 units.

3. Draw a diagonal line from corner to corner on the wrong side of two 2½" light #2 squares. Place each marked square on a 2½" black #1 square, right sides together. Sew ¼" from each side of the drawn line. Cut the units apart on the marked line and press to make four half-square-triangle units. Trim the units to measure 2" square.

Make 4 units.

4. Arrange and sew the units in three rows as shown. The light #1 triangles should be next to the green print triangles. Sew the rows together to complete the Ohio Star block. It should measure 5" square, including seam allowances.

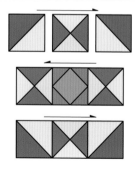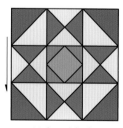

Make 1 block,
5" × 5".

SETTING BLOCKS

1. Follow step 3 of "Ohio Star Block" on page 59 using 2½" light #2 and black #1 squares. Make 12 half-square-triangle setting blocks and trim to measure 2" square. Repeat with two gold #2 squares to make four setting blocks.

Make 12 blocks.

Make 4 blocks.

2. Using the 3" light #2 and black #1 triangles, sew a light triangle to a black triangle as shown. Then sew a 2½" black #1 triangle to the unit to make a setting block. Trim to measure 2" square. Make four setting blocks.

Make 4 blocks.

NINE PATCH BLOCKS

1. Sew one 1" × 26" light #3 and two 1" × 26" red #1 strips together as shown to make a strip set that measures 2" × 26". Straighten the end and cut 24 segments, 1" × 2".

Make 1 strip set, 2" × 26".
Cut 24 segments, 1" × 2".

2. Sew two 1" × 14" light #3 strips and one 1" × 14" red #1 strip together as shown to make a strip set that measures 2" × 14". Straighten the end and cut 12 segments, 1" × 2".

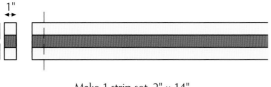

Make 1 strip set, 2" × 14".
Cut 12 segments, 1" × 2".

3. Arrange and sew the segments together as shown to make a Nine Patch block measuring 2" square, including seam allowances. Press the seams open. Make a total of 12 Nine Patch blocks.

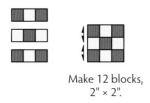

Make 12 blocks,
2" × 2".

PINWHEEL BLOCKS

1. Draw a diagonal line from corner to corner on the wrong side of two 1¾" light #2 squares. Place a marked square on a 1¾" blue square, right sides together. Sew ¼" from each side of the drawn line. Cut the unit apart on the marked line and press to make two half-square-triangle units. Trim the units to measure 1¼" square. Repeat with the second marked light square and a 1¾" green #2 square.

1¼" 1¼"
1¼" 1¼"

Make 2 of each unit.

2. Lay out and sew the half-square-triangle units in two rows, rotating and alternating them to form a pinwheel as shown. Join the rows to make a block measuring 2" square, including seam allowances. Press. Make a total of eight Pinwheel blocks.

Make 8 blocks,
2" × 2".

ASSEMBLING THE QUILT CENTER

Lay out the Ohio Star block, the setting blocks, the Pinwheel blocks, and the Nine Patch blocks as shown. Sew the units together in rows and then sections. Join the sections to create the quilt center. Press in alternating directions for opposing seams. The quilt center should measure 11" square, including seam allowances.

Quilt center,
11" × 11".

ADDING BORDER ONE

Referring to the adding borders diagram on page 63, sew a 1¼" × 11" black #1 border strip to each side of the quilt center; press. Then sew the 1¼" × 12½" black #1 strips to the top and bottom of the quilt; press. The quilt center should measure 12½" square, including seam allowances.

ADDING BORDER TWO

1. Draw a diagonal line from corner to corner on the wrong side of twelve 1¾" light #4 squares. Place a marked square on each of six blue 1¾" squares and six red #1 squares, right sides together. Sew ¼" from each side of the drawn line. Cut each unit apart on the marked line and press to make a total of 12 blue and 12 red half-square-triangle units. Trim to 1¼" square.

Make 12 of each unit.

2. Sew two 2¼" light #4 triangles to a blue half-square-triangle as shown; press.

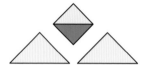

3. Sew two 1⅞" black #1 triangles to the triangle unit as shown to make a border unit that measures 1½" × 2½". Make a total of 12 units with blue triangles and 12 units with red triangles.

Make 12 of each unit,
1½" × 2½".

Slow and Steady

Take extra care when sewing the pieced triangle units. Match your points and raw edges and be sure to sew your seam perfectly straight. There are a lot of bias edges to deal with and sewing slowly may help you keep control.

4. Sew three red and three blue units together, alternating colors and beginning with a red unit. Make a total of four pieced borders measuring 1½" × 12½", including seam allowances. Sew a 1½" red #2 square to each end of two of the pieced borders to make the top and bottom borders, measuring 1½" × 14½".

Make 2 side borders,
1½" × 12½".

Make 2 top/bottom borders,
1½" × 14½".

5. Sew the two shorter pieced borders to the sides of the quilt center; press. Sew the top and bottom borders to the quilt center and press. The quilt should measure 14½" square, including seam allowances.

Adding borders 1 and 2

ADDING BORDER THREE

Sew the 1" × 14½" gold #3 border strips to the sides of the quilt center; press. Then sew the 1" × 15½" gold #3 strips to the top and bottom of the quilt; press. The quilt should measure 15½" square, including seam allowances.

ADDING BORDER FOUR

1. Referring to "Connector Corners" on page 74, draw a diagonal line from corner to corner on the wrong side of the 1¼" black #2 squares. Placed a marked square on one end of a 1¼" × 2" red #3 rectangle, right sides together. Stitch on the marked line. Press, making sure the raw edges of the triangle are aligned with the edges of the rectangle. Trim away the excess corner fabric, leaving a ¼" seam allowance. Press the triangle back in place. Place a marked square on the right side of the rectangle and repeat to make a flying-geese unit measuring 1¼" × 2", including seam allowances. Make a total of 80 units.

Make 80 units,
1¼" × 2".

2. Sew 20 flying-geese units together to make a border measuring 2" × 15½", including seam allowances; press. Make a total of four borders.

Make 4 borders,
2" × 15½".

3. Referring to step 3 of "Ohio Star Block" on page 59, make half-square-triangle units with two 2½" black #2 squares and two 2½" blue squares, drawing the diagonal line on the wrong side of the blue squares. Make a total of four half-square-triangle units and trim them to 2" square.

2"

2"

Make 4 units.

4. Referring to the quilt assembly diagram below, sew a flying-geese border to opposite sides of the quilt center, paying attention to the direction of the flying-geese units. Press. Sew a half-square-triangle unit to each end of the two remaining borders. Sew these to the top and bottom of the quilt center. Press. The quilt should measure 18½" square, including seam allowances.

ADDING BORDER FIVE

Sew a 3½" × 18½" black #2 border strip to each side of the quilt center; press. Then sew the black 3½" × 24½" strips to the top and bottom of the quilt; press. The quilt should measure 24½" square.

FINISHING THE QUILT

1. Make, sign, and date a label and attach to the quilt backing, if desired. For my label technique, see "Adding a Label" on page 76.

2. Layer the quilt top with batting and backing. Quilt by hand or by machine. My quilt is machine quilted with a fleur-de-lis pattern in both the dark and light fabrics of the center half-square-triangle units, the Ohio Star flying-geese units, and the block center unit. Point-to-point curves are stitched in the quarter-square-triangle units of the Ohio Star, the light prints of the Pinwheel blocks, and border 2. A diagonal line is quilted through the red prints of the Nine Patch blocks. The plain black and gold inner borders are quilted in the ditch. The black triangles of border 2 have a swirl in the center. A tiny three-petal design is quilted in the red flying-geese units and a feather design is stitched in the outer border.

3. Trim the excess batting and backing. Use the 2¼"-wide black #3 strips to make double-fold binding and sew the binding to the quilt. If you need additional help, go to ShopMartingale.com for free downloadable information.

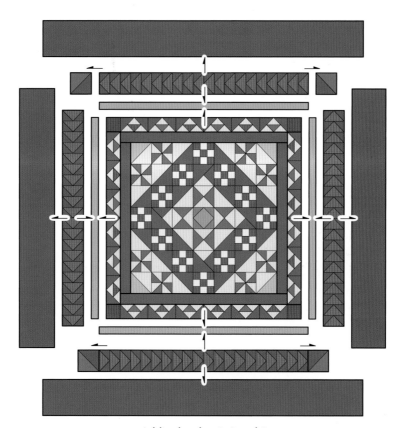

Adding borders 3, 4, and 5

Camp Independence

Inspired by an antique quilt, Camp Independence invites you to show your colors! Perfectly complementing the center stars, the half-square triangles marching briskly around the border suggest banners waving, flags flying, and an old-fashioned parade on a bright summer day.

QUILT SIZE: 21½" × 24½" | BLOCK SIZE: 3" × 3"

MATERIALS

Yardage is based on 42"-wide fabric.

1 yard of red print for blocks, setting squares, setting triangles, and borders

½ yard of blue print for blocks, borders, and binding

½ yard of light print for blocks and borders

¾ yard of fabric for backing

26" × 29" piece of batting

Designed by Pam Buda
Pieced by Debbie McClarence
Quilted by Ronda Dranter

CUTTING

From the light print, cut:
4 strips, 2" × 42"; crosscut into:
 48 rectangles, 1¼" × 2"
 38 squares 2" × 2"
2 strips, 1¼" × 42"; crosscut into 48 squares
 1¼" × 1¼"
2 strips, 1" × 42"; crosscut into:
 2 strips, 1" × 18½"
 2 strips, 1" × 16½"

From the blue print, cut:
3 strips, 2¼" × 42"
1 strip, 2" × 42"; crosscut into 19 squares, 2" × 2"
2 strips, 1¾" × 42"; crosscut into 24 squares
 1¾" × 1¾"
2 strips, 1¼" × 42"; crosscut into 48 squares
 1¼" × 1¼"

Continued on page 68

Continued from page 67

From the red print, cut:

1 strip, 5½" × 42"; crosscut into:

    3 squares, 5½" × 5½"; cut into quarters diagonally
to make 12 triangles (2 are extra)

    2 squares, 3" × 3"; cut in half diagonally to make
4 triangles

1 strip, 3½" × 42"; crosscut into 6 squares, 3½" × 3½"

4 strips, 2" × 42"; crosscut into 4 strips, 2" × 21½"

1 strip, 2" × 42"; crosscut into 19 squares, 2" × 2"

4 strips, 1¾" × 42"; crosscut *1 strip* into 24 squares,
1¾" × 1¾"

2 strips, 1¼" × 42"; crosscut into 48 squares,
1¼" × 1¼"

PINWHEEL UNITS

Press all seam allowances as indicated by the arrows.

1. Draw a diagonal line from corner to corner on the
wrong side of 24 red 1¾" squares. Place a marked
square on a blue 1¾" square, right sides together.
Sew ¼" from each side of the drawn line. Cut the
unit apart on the marked line and press to make
two half-square-triangle units. Trim the units to
measure 1¼" square. Make a total of 48 red/blue
half-square-triangle units.

Make 48 units.

2. Arrange and sew four half-square triangle units
together in pairs as shown. Sew the pairs together
to make pinwheel unit A measuring 2" square,
including seam allowances. Make six A units.

Make 6 A units,
2" × 2".

3. Repeat step 2, arranging the half-square-triangle
units in the opposite direction as shown to make
pinwheel unit B. Make six B units.

Make 6 B units,
2" × 2".

FLYING-GEESE UNITS

1. Referring to "Connector Corners" on page 74,
draw a diagonal line from corner to corner on
the wrong side of a red and a blue 1¼" square.
Place a marked red square on the left end of a
light 1¼" × 2" rectangle. Stitch on the marked
line. Press, making sure the raw edges of
the triangle are aligned with the edges of the
rectangle. Trim away the excess corner fabric,
leaving a ¼" seam allowance. Press the triangle
back in place. Place a marked blue square on
the right end of the rectangle; repeat to make
flying-geese unit A measuring 1¼" × 2", including
seam allowances. Make a total of 24 A units.

Make 24 A units,
1¼" × 2".

2. Repeat step 1, reversing the placement of the red
and blue squares. Make a total of 24 B units.

Make 24 B units,
1¼" × 2".

LEMOYNE STAR BLOCKS

1. Arrange and sew a pinwheel A unit, four flying-geese A units, and four light 1¼" squares in rows as shown. Sew the rows together and press to make a LeMoyne Star A block measuring 3½" square, including seam allowances. Make six A blocks.

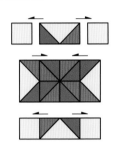
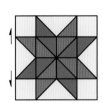

Make 6 A blocks,
3½" × 3½".

2. Repeat step 1, arranging a pinwheel B unit, four flying-geese B units, and four light 1¼" squares. Make six LeMoyne Star B blocks.

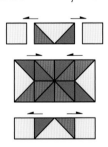
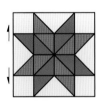

Make 6 B blocks,
3½" × 3½".

ASSEMBLING THE QUILT CENTER

1. Referring to the quilt assembly diagram above right, lay out the 12 LeMoyne Star blocks on point in four rows of three blocks each, alternating the A and B blocks across the horizontal rows. Add the red 3½" setting squares between the blocks; then add the red 5½" side setting triangles and 3" corner triangles. Sew the blocks and triangles into diagonal rows.

2. Sew the rows together. Press. The quilt center should measure approximately 13¼" × 17½", including seam allowances.

Quilt assembly

ADDING THE BORDERS

1. Measure the length of the quilt through the center; cut two strips to that measurement from a red 1¾" × 42" strip. Sew the strips to the sides of the quilt center. Measure the width of the quilt through the center, including the borders just added. Cut two strips to that measurement from the remaining red 1¾" × 42" strip. Sew the strips to the top and bottom. The quilt should measure about 15¾" × 20", including seam allowances.

2. Trim the quilt to measure 15½" × 18½". To do this, you will be trimming about ⅛" from each side and approximately ¾" from the top and ¾" from the bottom. After trimming, the red borders will no longer be of equal width. This is done to accommodate the pieced borders.

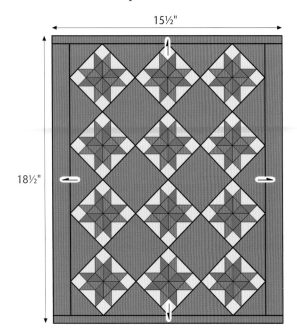

15½"

18½"

Add the inner borders and trim.

3. Sew the light 1" × 18½" border strips to the sides of the quilt center and then sew the light 1" × 16½" strips to the top and bottom. The quilt should measure 16½" × 19½", including seam allowances.

4. Draw a diagonal line from corner to corner on the wrong side of the 38 light 2" squares. Place a marked square on a red or a blue 2" square, right sides together. Sew ¼" from each side of the drawn lines. Cut the units apart on the marked line and press. Trim the units to measure 1½" square. Make a total of 38 red and 38 blue half-square-triangle units. (You'll have one extra half-square-triangle unit of each color.)

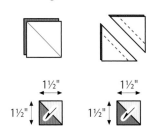

1½"   1½"

1½"   1½"

Make 38 units.   Make 38 units.

5. Arrange and sew ten red and nine blue half-square-triangle units together to make a left side border that measures 1½" × 19½", including seam allowances. Make a right side border with nine red and ten blue half-square-triangle units.

Make 1 left side border,
1½" × 19½".

Make 1 right side border,
1½" × 19½".

6. Sew nine red and nine blue half-square-triangle units together as shown to make the top border and sew nine red and nine blue half-square-triangle units together as shown to make the bottom border. The top and bottom borders should measure 1½" × 18½", including seam allowances.

Make 1 top border,
1½" × 18½".

Make 1 bottom border,
1½" × 18½".

7. Sew the side borders to the quilt center and then add the top and bottom borders. The quilt should measure 18½" × 21½", including seam allowances.

8. Sew the red print 2" × 21½" borders to the sides of the quilt and then add the remaining red print 2" × 21½" borders to the top and bottom. The quilt should measure 21½" × 24½".

Adding borders

FINISHING THE QUILT

1. Make, sign, and date a label and attach to the quilt backing, if desired. For my label technique, see "Adding a Label" on page 76.

2. Layer the quilt top with batting and backing. Quilt by hand or by machine. My quilt is machine quilted with feathered wreaths in the setting squares and feathers in the setting triangles. The LeMoyne stars are quilted in the ditch. A wave design is quilted in the red border. Circular pearls are quilted in the light border with point-to-point curves in the half-square-triangle units. A curved line and stars are quilted in the red outer border.

3. Trim the excess batting and backing. Use the blue 2¼"-wide strips to make double-fold binding and sew the binding to the quilt. If you need additional details, go to ShopMartingale.com for free downloadable information.

Quiltmaking Techniques

As we go through our quilting journey, it's often those little hints and tricks we pick up along the way that make our quilting experience better. I've worked hard to improve my piecing skills, which has made every quilt all the more enjoyable to put together. I revel in seeing my blocks measure what they should, I fist-pump when all my star and flying-geese points are perfect, and I do a happy dance when a pieced border fits just right. It's satisfying to see our piecing skills improve and our work get better and better.

Here are just some of the hints and pointers that have helped me become a better quiltmaker and have made my piecing journey all the more enjoyable. I hope you find some tips that will enhance your experience.

MY FABRIC CHOICES

I'm a traditional quilter and I adore historic prints. However, I don't consider myself a reproduction purist, and I don't like *every* nineteenth-century color or print. Like many of you, I choose the fabrics that really appeal to me, and that's exactly how I design my reproduction fabrics for Marcus Fabrics.

Tone-on-tone prints are a staple in my fabric stash because they can often calm a quilt and give the eye a place to rest. But, it's the prints with multiple colors that make my heart skip a beat and add interest to a quilt. They can be harder to find, so when I see a multicolored print I like, I buy it right away.

If you find a fabric you like but don't have an immediate project in mind, you might not know how much to buy. If I'm just collecting, I buy ⅓-yard cuts. If I really love a fabric, I buy a full yard. If I think a fabric would make a great sashing or border, I buy 2½ yards so I can cut four strips, 10" × the length of the fabric. The strips are long enough to fit any quilt up to king size, so I'm sure to have plenty.

STARCHING FABRICS

I've been treating my fabric yardage with starch or spray sizing for more than 15 years now. I believe it plays a big part in the success of every quilt I make. While it takes some time to apply, the benefits are great.

Starching is all about fabric control, simple as that. Starched, stiff fabric goes where you want it to go and stays in place. It doesn't move as easily under your ruler when cutting, it goes where you want it to when piecing, and pressing is crisp and clean. What's not to love? All I ask is that you give it a try and make one block. I think you'll notice the difference in cutting, piecing, and pressing while you work.

There's one very important caveat to remember. Only starch or size *fabric yardage*. This means do it before cutting. Any liquid that touches dry fabric will begin to shrink it a little bit. If you have cut fabrics or pieced units made of unstarched fabric, don't spray with starch—otherwise you might get warping or shrinkage. But, if you've starched or sized your *yardage*, you can add more at any stage of the piecing. I also don't recommend starching or spray sizing any precuts, such as charm packs or 10" squares.

I add starch to my fabric yardage using two methods: in the washing machine and spraying the fabric directly.

Starching in the Washing Machine

I use a liquid starch such as Sta-Flo for this method, but you can use your favorite.

1. Put up to 4 yards of same-colored fabrics in the washer and set it for a small load and a delicate cycle. Rinse in cold water and spin the fabric so that it will better absorb the starch mixture and allow it to be worked into the entire piece of fabric.

2. In a mixing bowl, combine 1½ cups of Sta-Flo liquid starch and 4 cups of water. (This ratio creates a medium stiffness.)

3. Place the damp fabric in a clean tub or basin and pour the starch mixture over the fabric. Squeeze and work the starch into all the yards of fabric.

4. Return the fabric to the washer and spin (not rinse and spin) the fabric to remove excess liquid.

5. Hang the fabric to dry and then press with a steam iron to remove wrinkles.

Starching with a Spray Can

When spraying fabric, I prefer to use Magic Sizing. I use Magic Sizing for both scraps (any size) and yardage, too. You can try different brands on the market and see which you like best.

1. Cover your work surface with an old towel to absorb the extra liquid.

2. Lay the fabric out on the towel and thoroughly soak it with sizing. Be sure to soak the fabric evenly. I spray until the sizing nearly drips out of it when I pick it up.

3. Set the fabric aside to rest. I place same-color fabrics in a pile while I spray more fabric. Giving the fabrics time to rest allows the sizing to penetrate the fibers.

4. Hang the fabric to dry and then press with a steam iron to remove the wrinkles.

Now you're ready to begin working with the fabric and discover the control you have. It's a good idea, but not essential, to wash the completed project to remove any residues from the starch.

MEASURE, MEASURE, MEASURE!

Accuracy can only be achieved by checking and double-checking your measurements. It's by measuring each stitched unit that we know if we're accurate or not. When each unit and block measures *exactly* what it should, your quilt will be easy to piece.

As you piece and create the units, blocks, and rows for your quilt, check to be sure the measurements are accurate. If not, figure out why. Did you miscut the pieces? Is your seam allowance too small or too large? Are the two fabrics misaligned along the raw edges? If you have an error, rip out the seam and try again. If you fix any problems as you go, quilt assembly will go smoothly, your points will match, and your borders and quilt top will lie flat. Time spent measuring is time well spent, and the quilting experience will be more enjoyable as a result.

FABRIC ALIGNMENT

One of the easiest ways to lose accuracy is by sewing fabrics together when the raw edges are not perfectly aligned. Think of it this way: when you cut two layers of fabric with an acrylic ruler and rotary cutter, those two fabric edges are never more perfectly aligned than when they are cut at the same time. Each and every time you sew two fabrics together, be it units for a block, one block to another block, or a quilt center to a border, the raw edges of both fabrics should be evenly aligned.

CONNECTOR CORNERS

Connector-corner squares, or sew-and-flip corners, revolutionized the way we construct some quilt blocks. This technique facilitates fun and easy piecing, and it has allowed me to design uniquely original blocks and other quilt elements. A connector-corner square used in a unit, block, sashing strip, and even a border can yield very striking results.

While piecing a connector-corner square is simple, there are four principles I follow for perfect results.

1. When instructed to draw a diagonal line from corner to corner on the wrong side of a square, be sure your pencil or marker—not your ruler—goes from point to point.

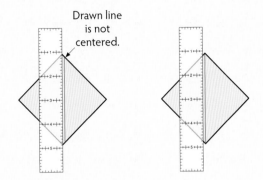

Drawn line is not centered.

2. Be sure to perfectly align the raw edges of the marked square with the base square or rectangle (see "Fabric Alignment" on page 74). For a square-in-a-square unit, the marked square and base square are aligned on two sides. For a flying-geese unit, the marked square and base rectangle are aligned on three sides.

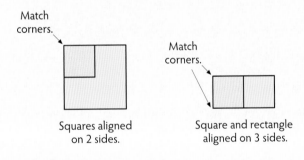

Match corners.

Match corners.

Squares aligned on 2 sides.

Square and rectangle aligned on 3 sides.

3. When instructed to sew on the drawn line, sew one or two threads on the seam-allowance side of the line. This is the equivalent of a scant ¼" seam allowance and allows for the few threads of fabric lost in the fold after pressing.

4. Directions often say to trim away the excess fabric of the seam allowance and press. I recommend that you do this in reverse order—press and then trim. By pressing first, you can check the accuracy of the connector-corner triangle. You want to be sure that the raw edges of the triangle are perfectly aligned with the raw edges of the base piece.

If the triangle doesn't reach the raw edge of the base piece, the points will not be perfect, the angles will not align, and your unit will not measure what it should. If the triangle extends beyond the base piece, you will lose the points of the unit. The seam of the connector corner is usually short, so it's easy to rip it out and do over. When the connector-corner triangle is perfectly aligned with the base piece, you know it measures what it should, and you can confidently trim away the middle and base fabrics to reduce bulk. So always press first, check for accuracy, and then trim the excess fabric for perfect connector corners every time!

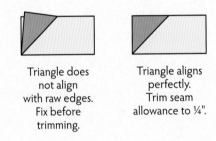

Triangle does not align with raw edges. Fix before trimming.

Triangle aligns perfectly. Trim seam allowance to ¼".

MAKE IT LARGER AND TRIM

By now, you understand how strongly I believe that accuracy produces great results. Any time I can make a unit or block larger than needed and trim it to perfection, I do! Innovative designers are coming up with new and wonderful ways to do this every year, and I'm all for it.

When making half-square-triangle units, adding ⅛" to the size of the square is enough to allow for trimming a little extra fabric, resulting in a perfect unit. The slightly larger size of the square won't alter the quilt's yardage requirements. (If you choose to make your units even larger, in order to have more to trim, you certainly can. However, additional yardage may be required for your project.) When making a finished 3" × 3" half-square-triangle unit, you would usually cut 3⅞" squares from two different fabrics. I simply increase the size of the squares by ⅛" and cut 4" squares instead. Using finished 3" × 3" units as an example, here's how I create perfect half-square-triangle units every time.

1. Cut a 4" square from each of two different fabrics. Draw a diagonal line from corner to corner on the wrong side of the lighter square. Place the marked square on top of the darker square, right sides together. Sew ¼" from both sides of the drawn line. Cut the unit apart on the marked line. Press as directed in the project instructions, usually toward the darker fabric.

2. Using a 3½"-square ruler and a mat, place the 45° line of the ruler on top of the diagonal seam. Move the ruler up and down along the diagonal seam until a little fabric extends beyond the ruler on all four sides.

3. Use a rotary cutter to trim two sides of the unit. Without moving the ruler, rotate the mat and unit 90° and trim the remaining two sides of the unit.

ADDING A LABEL

I add a label to every quilt I make. As a collector of antique quilts, I would dearly love to know the provenance of each quilted treasure and the background of the quiltmaker. If only those old quilts could tell their own story! By labeling my quilts, I'm passing on their story to future generations. My descendants will know the *who, what, when, where,* and *why* of every quilt and the love I put into every stitch.

To create my labels, I use a computer and printer, and I choose a beige tone-on-tone fabric that was either used in the quilt top or that coordinates nicely with the quilt fabrics.

1. Using an 8½" × 11" sheet of heavy-duty freezer paper (available at your local quilt shop), press a slightly larger piece of the desired label fabric to the wax side of the freezer paper until it's firmly affixed. Using an acrylic ruler and rotary cutter, trim the fabric even with the paper. (I often prepare several of these to have on hand.)

2. Using your computer, create a document with all of the information you'd like to include in the label. I always center the text on the page. You can get creative with different fonts and sizes, adding clip art and photos if you like. I also make the font bold so that more ink is printed on the fabric. To save fabric and time, I usually create and print two quilt labels at once on an 8½" × 11" page.

3. To be sure the fabric is firmly adhered to the paper, press the fabric/freezer paper with a dry iron just before feeding it into your inkjet printer, and then hit print.

4. I use a fine-point Sharpie marker to add my signature for a personal touch, and then I thoroughly press the entire label with a dry iron to set the ink.

5. Use a rotary cutter and ruler to trim the label at least 1" from each end of the longest line of text. Remove the freezer paper from the back.

6. Using scraps from the quilt project, add a fabric frame around all four sides of the label. I often use one fabric for the frame, but sometimes I use four different scraps. You can also add leftover blocks and scraps to make a more creative label.

7. Turn the raw edges of the frame under and press. Position the label on the backing fabric so it will be in a central spot under the quilt and away from the quilt edge. I use Roxanne's Glue-Baste-It to glue the label to the backing fabric. Then I use monofilament thread and a blind hem stitch to machine stitch the label to the backing fabric before layering and basting.

I find this method the easiest and most secure, as the label is quilted right into the quilt and would not be easy to remove. You can also write the information for your label by hand and then frame, glue, and sew it to your backing as described. No matter what method you choose, be sure to tell the story of the quilt to future generations. They'll be so glad you did!

SINGLE-FOLD BINDING

Normally, I use double-fold binding for my quilts because the double fold holds up well to all the cuddling, love, and use that quilts get in my family. For a few of the sweet little quilts in this book, though, double-fold binding is too bulky. Instead, a narrow single-fold binding is the way to go, and it's easy to do. I cut 2"-wide binding strips for single-fold binding and 2¼"-wide strips for double-fold binding. If you need information about making and applying double-fold binding, visit Martingale.com/HowtoQuilt. To make single-fold binding, follow these steps.

1. Join the strips end to end to make a long piece of binding. Press the seam allowances open.

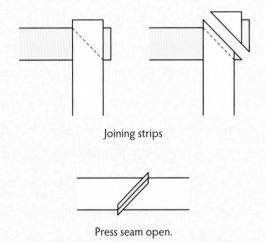

Joining strips

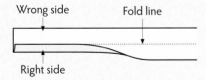

Press seam open.

2. Fold the strip in half lengthwise, wrong sides together, and press. Open the strip with the wrong side of the fabric facing up. On one side, fold the raw edge of the strip toward the center, aligning the raw edge with the fold line, and press.

Wrong side   Fold line

Right side

3. Trim the backing and batting even with the quilt top.

4. Starting in the middle of one side and using a ¼" seam allowance, stitch the binding to the quilt. Keep the raw edges even with the quilt-top

edge. Begin stitching 4" to 5" from the start of the binding. End the stitching ¼" from the corner of the quilt and backstitch.

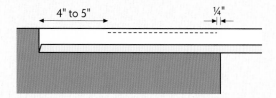

5. Turn the quilt so you'll be stitching along the next side. Fold the binding up and away from the quilt; then fold it back down onto itself, even with the raw edge of the quilt top.

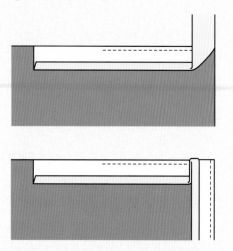

6. Stitch from the fold of the binding along the second edge of the quilt top, stopping ¼" from the corner as before. Repeat the stitching and mitering process on the remaining edges and corners.

7. Stop stitching about 5" from the point where you started attaching the binding; backstitch. Remove the quilt from the machine. Overlap the beginning and ending tails of the binding. Mark a 2" overlap and trim each end of the binding at the marked points.

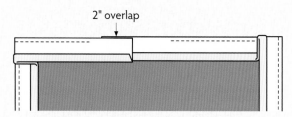

8. Open the folds of the two ends of the binding and overlap the ends at right angles, right sides together. Pin the ends together and draw a diagonal line between the points where the strips intersect. Sew the binding ends together along the drawn line. Trim the excess corner fabric, leaving a ¼" seam allowance. Finger-press the seam allowances open. Then refold the binding strip and sew it in place on the quilt.

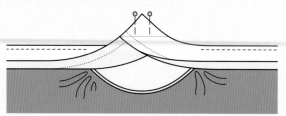

Draw diagonal line.
Pin ends together.

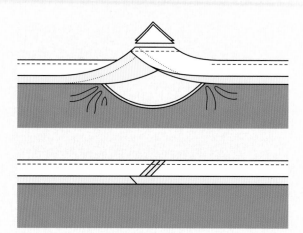

9. Fold the binding over the raw edges of the quilt to the back, with the folded edge covering the row of machine stitching. Hand stitch in place, mitering the corners.

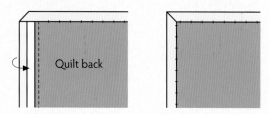

Quilt back

Acknowledgments

As it is with any project of this size, I have many people to thank for the work that goes on behind the scenes to make my quilts and this book possible. I am so grateful for your advice, help, and understanding through the years.

My heartfelt thanks to the entire staff at Martingale for being excited about my book of small quilts and for their expert guidance throughout the writing process. It's exciting, and at the same time terrifying, to even think about writing a book. You make the whole experience enjoyable and I am honored and grateful to be part of the Martingale family of authors.

Over the years, I have been blessed with ideas for every size of quilt. I can't possibly piece them all myself, so I want to thank my stitching friends Debbie McClarence and Pat Creehan for piecing several of the quilts in this book. I'm proud to own quilts that you've pieced.

Generally, I don't quilt any of my own quilts. I give nearly all of my quilts to my friend and quilter extraordinaire Ronda Dranter. She works closely with me to choose just the right quilting designs in keeping with the traditional feel of each quilt, plus she does her best to accommodate a very tight schedule.

Additionally, in this book you'll see the quilting talent of Valerie Krueger (Quilting by Val) and Marcella Pickett and Margie Love (Crooked Creek Quilting). Thank you for making my quilts the very best they can be.

I simply don't know what I would do without my friend and coworker Debbie McClarence. She fills orders, maintains my website, cuts kits and fabrics, tests patterns, and pieces many of my quilts. She keeps things running smoothly, allowing me to concentrate on designing quilts and fabrics, and keeps us laughing while we do it all.

Saving the best for last, I would not have a business, or be able to do what I love, if not for the most important people in my life. To my husband, Ed, who has always believed in me and offered unwavering encouragement from the very beginning. To my daughter, Nicki, who has done a myriad of different things to help me over the years; it's been great fun working with you and going on road trips with you. And to my son, Ryan, I wholeheartedly thank you for hauling innumerable boxes up and down the stairs and packing my car with even more boxes for countless road trips. (He now has a great aversion to boxes!) I will pay for therapeutic massages! You're all my reason for living and I love you all to the moon and back.

About the Author

Pam Buda began her quiltmaking journey in 1997. Before long she was designing original quilts, and in 2004, began self-publishing her patterns under her company name, Heartspun Quilts. She loves traditional blocks and is inspired by her collection of nineteenth-century quilts.

Pam also has a love of early American history, and years of reading about what daily life was like for eighteenth- and nineteenth-century women allowed her to combine her two loves of history and quilting into her well-known Prairie Women's Sewing Circle Club, hosted by participating quilt shops since 2009. More recently, she created the very popular Circa 1880 Nine Patch Club, also available through participating quilt shops.

In 2011, Pam's love of historic fabrics led her to begin designing fabrics for Marcus Fabrics in her signature prairie style. She designs quilts and sewing projects of all sizes that have been seen in *American Patchwork and Quilting*, *Primitive Quilts and Projects*, and *Quiltmaker* magazines. Her first book for Martingale, *Vintage Patchwork*, was released in 2018. She also enjoys traveling. She presents lectures and workshops to guilds and at quilt shops, quilt shows, retreats, and on quilting cruises.

Pam lives in a suburb of Chicago with her husband, Ed, and grown kids, Nicki and Ryan, and their Yorkie, Bella. Visit HeartspunQuilts.com to learn more. Follow Pam on Facebook, Instagram, and Pinterest (@heartspunquilts).